Pencil, Paper and Stars

Pencil, Paper and Stars

The Handbook of Traditional and Emergency Navigation

ALASTAIR BUCHAN

John Wiley & Sons, Ltd

Copyright © 2008   Alastair Buchan

Published by   John Wiley & Sons Ltd, The Atrium, Southern Gate, Chichester,
                      West Sussex PO19 8SQ, England
                      Telephone   (+44) 1243 779777

Email (for orders and customer service enquiries): cs-books@wiley.co.uk
Visit our Home Page on www.wiley.com

Other Wiley Editorial Offices

John Wiley & Sons Inc., 111 River Street, Hoboken, NJ 07030, USA

Jossey-Bass, 989 Market Street, San Francisco, CA 94103-1741, USA

Wiley-VCH Verlag GmbH, Boschstr. 12, D-69469 Weinheim, Germany

John Wiley & Sons Australia Ltd, 42 McDougall Street, Milton, Queensland 4064, Australia

John Wiley & Sons (Asia) Pte Ltd, 2 Clementi Loop #02-01, Jin Xing Distripark, Singapore 129809

John Wiley & Sons Canada Ltd, 22 Worcester Road, Etobicoke, Ontario, Canada, M9W 1LI

Wiley also publishes its books in a variety of electronic formats. Some content that appears in print may not be
available in electronic books.

Library of Congress Cataloging-in-Publication Data

Buchan, Alastair.
    Pencil, paper and stars : the handbook of traditional and emergency navigation / Alastair Buchan.
       p.   cm.
    Includes index.
    ISBN 978-0-470-51652-2 (pbk. : alk. paper)
1. Yachting.   2. Navigation.   I. Title.
    GV813.B785   2008
    623.89–dc22

                                                              2007035528

British Library Cataloguing in Publication Data

A catalogue record for this book is available from the British Library

ISBN 978-0-470-51652-2 (PB)

Typeset in 10/15pt Futura by Aptara Inc., New Delhi, India
Printed and bound in Singapore by Markono

Contents

An excellent art

Navigation is that excellent Art, which demonstrateth by infallible conclusions, how a sufficient Ship may be conducted the shortest good way from place to place, by Table and Travers.

John Davis, *The Seaman's Secrets*, 1594

Electronics took its time killing traditional navigation. The first hint of its intentions was in 1906 when the Italians Bellini and Tosi found how to determine the direction from which radio signals were transmitted. By the end of the 1940s radio navigation had grown to include Consol, Decca, Loran-C (the Russians had their version called Chayka), and Omega, the son of a 1940s development called Radux and the first worldwide positioning system. It even had its own differential system for improved accuracy and was switched off only in 1997. It is hard to believe that only 30 years ago hi-tech, electronic navigation for most yachtsmen was donning a set of headphones and waving a glorified transistor radio vaguely towards a radio beacon in the hope of obtaining a bearing on a magnetic compass that could be plotted on a paper chart.

The introduction of inertia navigation was ignored by the leisure sailor and the arrival of satellite navigation gave no hint of its future dominance. With only one, often doubtful, fix every half hour or so and a cumbersome, parsimonious display, the Transit system hardly seemed worth the expense and certainly no reason to throw away your sextant.

Navigational calculators were expensive and rarely found on yachts. A few enthusiasts wrote simple navigation programmes for the handful of calculators that could be persuaded to remember a few keystrokes. Primitive by today's standards and less than user friendly, these were the ancestors of those managing today's GPS sets.

There were no digital charts. Positions were plotted on paper, just as they had been since the Egyptians invented papyrus.

Navigation stubbornly remained more art than science, heavy with traditions. Innovation, when finally accepted, came in small, genteel steps building carefully on what had gone before. The sextant's lineage goes back over 2,000 years to the astrolabe. Robert Hooke showed the prototype of the modern sextant to the Royal Society in 1666. Isaac Newton described his notion for a double reflecting sextant to a Royal Society meeting in1699. Both ideas sank without trace. It was 1731 before Thomas Godfrey in America, and John Hadley, a London instrument maker, simultaneously and independently re-invented the double reflecting quadrant. In the summer of 1837, over a century later, Captain Thomas H Sumner accidentally developed the celestial position line but it was 1875 before Captain, later Admiral, Marc St Hilaire cracked the maths behind the altitude-difference method of establishing a position line, and the middle of the 20th century was approaching before short method tables were published.

The rotator log replaced the medieval log ship towards the end of the 19th century. Around the 1930s the micrometer drum superseded the vernier scale on sextants. In the late 1950s, the echo-sounder finally took over from the lead line. Hardly revolutionary progress. Well into the 1980s, navigators like Cook or Bligh would have had no difficulty in coming up to speed on the latest techniques and then showing us how it should be done.

In an overnight coup, the microchip deposed centuries of tradition and changed everything. Watches, so accurate that in the past they would have been cherished as top end chronometers, became so cheap that they were disposable. LCD screens provided detailed information in easily understood language that superseded the analogue display. Plotters, digital charts, digital compasses, radios, autohelms, radars, and, soon after it went fully operational in 1995, GPS, all quickly became commonplace on the smallest yacht.

The computer in every instrument began networking with every other, and displaying more information than any reasonable navigator was able to use. Modern navigation requires no prior knowledge or skill. If you can send a text message then you can navigate. The distinction between coastal and ocean navigation, novice and expert, amateur and professional, vanished. Knowing why or understanding how it is done is unimportant – irrelevant. Since May 1998, the United States Naval Academy has stopped running courses on celestial navigation. The sextant is dead. Long live the microchip!

There is a downside. Electronic navigation makes the divine right of kings look like democracy in action. Instruments talk, but only to their equals and then announce decisions set in tablets of stone. Their proclamations are assumed accurate to several decimal places and their absolute reliability is unquestioned. Cross checking by traditional methods reveals only gross errors and since computers never err, why bother? So we no longer cross check, and age-old knowledge is forgotten.

But what happens when your electronic wizardry abdicates and leaves you alone with silent, blank screens upon an empty sea? After checking its connections and giving an encouraging thump you can do little more. Modern instruments are impervious to user repair. Why they fail is irrelevant. The fact is you are in the middle of nowhere and want to go home. The question is, how?

The kneejerk, textbook solution of digging out a paper chart and sharpening a pencil works brilliantly in the clubhouse, but unless you remember long-forgotten skills, have a clockwork log and magnetic compass you are going nowhere. Bar room knowledge may take you clear of the yacht club but before long you won't know where you are, how you got there, or how to return in time to buy your round. You need 'Crash Bag' (emergency) Navigation. The chances are it will get you to the bar on time and with a good tale to tell.

This book explains the principles involved in finding your way without instruments, and how to make simple instruments from materials you have on board. But you will find no answers, simple or otherwise. No formulaic solution can cover every situation. It is up to you to use the principles and techniques described in this book in a way that meets your circumstances. We modern navigators may not be as accurate, skilful or confident as those who learned these techniques through a long apprenticeship and used them every day, but we would have to be really slow not to learn enough to dig ourselves out of a hole and reach port.

Another kind of sailing

Positive Waves

Picture This

Keep It Simple

Proper Preparations

. . . three kindes of Sayling, Horizontal, Paradoxal, and Sayling upon a Great Circle
John Davis, *The Seaman's Secrets*, 1594

The techniques that once made piloting, dead reckoning and celestial navigation separate skills, are history. Nowadays navigation depends on accessing detailed and accurate data provided by an array of electronic devices that do not care if you are inshore, offshore, or in the middle of nowhere. But take these clever instruments away and the flow of data dries up, and we are lost unless we find some other way of acquiring the information that will allow us to continue on our way.

It can be done and has been done for thousands of years. Sailing without electronic instruments demands more of the navigator. He or she is no longer a button pusher but a combination of a mathematician, astronomer, biologist, meteorologist, cartographer, and geographer. It is daunting, but the biggest challenge is in acquiring or re-acquiring a mindset for another kind of sailing.

Positive Waves

Always think positive. A lack of instrumentation and charts is not a disaster. You are not inventing the wheel. Sailors have been navigating without instruments far longer than they have with them. They have even sailed round the world without them. Take comfort in the fact that you are not the first.

Accept Uncertainty

Be happy living with uncertainty. GPS has accustomed us to pinpoint our positions accurately all of the time, anywhere and everywhere. At one time, knowing your position to within a handful of metres was only possible if you had correctly identified and taken bearings or transits on several charted features. Unless you were anchored, the position had a half-life measured in minutes. The further you travelled the less certain your position. You were not lost, but where you were became an educated guess rather than a certainty taken to several decimal places.

Make Mistakes

Uncertainty means your position contains unknown errors. The only certainty is that you are not where you think. Sometimes a known error is better. You still do not know your precise position but at least you are making mistakes of your choosing.

Picture This

Digital navigators have been known to carefully log their vessel's GPS coordinates and minutes later run aground. They have failed to relate this information to the real world. Always doubtful of his position, a Crash Bag Navigator must remain spatially aware and keep a plot running in his head. In other words, he must have a mental picture of where the boat is in relation to the world about it.

You do this all the time. When travelling between home and work, at any point on the journey you can point towards your home, destination, or places in between, without any hesitation. You know where you are without looking at a map.

Similarly, the Crash Bag Navigator knows what course he's steering and what speed he's making. He always has in mind a fair approximation of the boat's position and its relationship to landmarks and hazards. He uses as many independent ways as possible to check his direction, position, and speed. Each check gives a slightly different answer but they should all lead to more or less the same position.

Keep It Simple

At one time, nautical ambitions more or less kept pace with navigational skills. You dared not sail across the bay and lose sight of land without being sure you could find terra firma again. Ocean passages waited until you had mastered astro-navigation.

With GPS, you can buy a boat on Monday and start out across the Atlantic on Tuesday. The occasion when you lose your instruments may be your first time at sea without their comfort blanket around you.

It is a steep learning curve. Keep it simple. Always chose the easy option. Prioritise the tasks facing you. Do them one at a time, deliberately, slowly, and check progress before moving onto the next task.

Proper Preparations

It is a fundamental truth that performance in any field is directly proportional to the preparations and training made beforehand. Lay the foundations for Crash Bag Navigation before you need it. You should not be trying it for the first time five minutes after your instruments die. Every passage plan should be prepared and made bearing in mind the possibility that Crash Bag Navigation might be needed.

Although there should be no difference between theory and practice, it would be prudent to take every opportunity to practise the ideas described in this book. You not only gain proficiency and a good understanding of the degree of accuracy you can expect, but learn to allow for inaccuracies.

If you live by the plotter then it is important to have an up-to-date written record of your position in a paper log, or as a plot on a paper chart. Without this you will have to guess where you are when you begin Crash Bag Navigation. It also helps to have written down (or printed out) the coordinates of the waypoints you intended to use.

Greater than the Whole

Although this book deals with topics separately, the trick is in putting them together. The sum of the parts is greater than the whole. Sometimes an insignificant, almost overlooked and apparently irrelevant detail in the distant outfield completes the picture. The Crash Bag Navigator is a ravenous and omnivorous collector of data.

The first navigators

Once cavemen developed a navigational methodology it was not long before this methodology became formalised with certificates of competence, and a range of gadgets all promising to make it easy. It would be wrong to think of the early navigators as uncivilised, uneducated, unsophisticated, unqualified and fearful of losing sight of land.

The distribution of finds of Irish Bronze Age gold ornaments showed that there was a healthy trade between Ireland, mainland Europe, Scotland and Denmark. Any way in which you retrace those routes involves some wild water sailing and serious navigation.

In the fourth century BCE, Herodotus wrote that when you were in 11 fathoms (this is a misprint for 100 fathoms) and found yellow mud on the lead then you were one day's sail from Alexandria. Mud from the Nile extends about 60 miles offshore, and soundings of 100 fathoms puts you some 50 nautical miles offshore. Coincidentally, the Minoans had a harbour at Knossus on the south coast of Crete whose only purpose was to trade with Africa, a good two days' sail across open sea.

Around 500 BCE Hanno, a Carthaginian, took 60 ships down the west coast of Africa, colonising as he went. He reached the region that is modern Sierra Leone. Even earlier, in 605 BCE Pharaoh Necho II, upset by failure in his war against Nebuchadnezzar and keen to secure his place in history, commissioned a Phoenician fleet to sail round Africa. They sailed down the east coast, round the Cape of Good Hope, up the west coast and back along the Mediterranean to Egypt.

This is a voyage of about 16 000 nautical miles and it took three years. Considering they stopped ashore for a few months each year to grow crops, they were either putting up eye-watering performances, or they had the capability to make long offshore passages, navigationally unequalled for many centuries.

Around 340 BCE another Phoenician, Pytheas of Massalia (present-day Marseilles) explored the Arctic Ocean and reached Utima Thule. Wherever that was, getting there involved offshore passages in some of the world's most inhospitable seas. Pytheas also invented an accurate method of calculating latitude using a calibrated sundial, theorised over the relationship between tides and the phases of the moon, and attempted to determine the position of true north.

On his return he documented his voyage in *Peritou Okeanou* (On the Ocean), which was lost. Fortunately, other writers drew upon it and we know Pytheas estimated the coastline of Britain to be 45,000 stades. Using the best guess we have about the length of a stade Pytheas made Britain's coastline 4,800 miles as against our figure of 4,710 miles.

In 146 BCE, Eudoxus of Cyzicus on his second voyage from Egypt to India was blown ashore below Cape Guardafui (then called the Cape of Spices) in Somalia off the Horn of Africa. There he found a wooden prow, carved with a horse's head, floating in the water. On his return to Carthage, he discovered that this was identical to those found on ships from Cadiz and Morocco. Did some navigator make it into the Indian Ocean a thousand years before Vasco Da Gama?

In about 100 BCE, the Roman geographer Statius Sebosus claimed that sailing for 40 days from the Gorgades brought you to the Hesperides, the legendary islands beyond the Atlantic Ocean. Some claim that the Gorgades are the Cape Verde Isles. If so, the next stop west is the Caribbean. On his third journey to the New World it took Columbus 33 days to sail between the Cape Verde Islands and the Caribbean. Was someone making transatlantic round trips 1600 years before Columbus? If so, who? Sadly Sebosus does not say.

Pliny the Elder in about 50 CE related the tides to the phases of the moon. Sometime around 700 CE, the Venerable Bede, sitting in his monastic cell by the River Wear in North-east England, described the tides round the British coast. Bede's work was used by seamen into the 17th century.

About 4000 years ago, on the far side of the world, the Polynesians began sailing the Pacific. Polynesian sea lanes have been correlated to the flight paths of migrating birds. Some believe that Polynesian explorers were great bird watchers, and that when they set out to explore it was to discover land that they were almost sure was there to be found. As they had no iron, they did not have magnetic compasses, but instead evolved a navigation system that needed neither instruments, nor charts as the west understood them. Their system survived more or less intact into the 19th century, and on a diminishing scale, into the early 20th century.

It is possible that some of their voyages were accidental, forced on them by heavy weather, but most were not. When they discovered an island accidentally, those who did so were not lost, for they found their way home with sufficient information for others to retrace their steps.

Closer to home and prior to 1492 the Caribs, Mayans and other tribes in the Caribbean sailed amongst the islands, and to and from the mainlands of North, Central and South America.

The expertise that made these early voyages possible is not completely lost. When John C Voss was sailing across the Pacific in his 30-foot *Tilikum* in September 1901 the boat was pooped 1200 miles from Sydney. He lost his companion and only compass overboard. Unfazed, he steered by the sun, moon, stars and swell to reach Sydney 22 days later. His confidence in his Crash Bag Navigation was so great that 15 minutes after noting that he should see 'Sidney light before long', he did.

In the 1960s, using Polynesian techniques, David Lewis sailed from Tahiti to New Zealand and made landfall within 30 miles of his destination. Between 1982 and 1984 Martin Creamer in *Gold Star* made one of the greatest circumnavigations ever by sailing round the world without using any instruments, not even a watch. Starting and ending at Cape May Harbor USA he called at Cape Town, Hobart, Sydney Whangora, and Port Stanley in the Falkland Islands.

It is unlikely the achievements of early navigators were lucky accidents. We know of Phoenician voyages, although not how they navigated, but to argue they did not develop a sophisticated navigational methodology is to believe they learnt nothing from centuries of voyaging. Look how far our own navigational skills have come in the last 500 years.

More to the point, early navigators probably had instruments. We think otherwise because we do not know about them or would not recognise them if we saw them. Sea power has always represented political power and wealth. Its skills and tools were jealously guarded secrets. Evidence of their existence was not left around for passers-by to pick up. This is still true today. Ask any military organisation for details of its latest navigational gizmos and you receive a bland and probably misleading answer.

Around 150 BCE the Greeks had a mechanical computer capable of predicting the movement of the sun, the moon, and some planets, as well as being able to add, subtract, multiply, and divide. Its remains were found in 1901 aboard a shipwreck. It took over a century to work out what it was. The Greeks also knew about the astrolabe and had star catalogues. The Pharaohs used sundials and knew the earth was spherical. They even measured its diameter pretty accurately. Devices for measuring the altitude of celestial bodies have been around for thousands of years. It is presumptuous to assume this knowledge was not used at sea.

Lead line apart, the first instrument to come into widespread maritime use was the compass. It possibly appeared in several places at about the same time as the characteristics of lodestone were widely known. The first mention of the compass in the west was by an Englishman Alexander Neckham. In his 1187 book *De Utensilibus* (On Instruments) he described a needle that swung on a point and showed the direction of north. This is a dry, pivoting compass needle so it is possible that the simpler, floating compass needle was in existence earlier than that.

Almost from the beginning, it was noted that compasses did not point to true north. Variation was empirically calculated in the 15th century. Around 1600 William Gilbert, physician to Queen Elizabeth I of England, suggested the difference was because the earth was behaving like a magnet, with its magnetic poles some distance away from its geographic ones.

In 1405, the Chinese began a series of voyages to establish trading routes throughout Micronesia, India, and the east coast of Africa. According to Gavin Menzies, the voyages peaked between 1421 and 1423 when four Chinese fleets circumnavigated the world, charting it as they went, using this information to produce an accurate world map in 1428.

Charts, pilots, tide tables, traverse tables, and almanacs have been used for centuries. Techniques for measuring time and angles, calculating position, speed, and direction have been around even longer. The solutions the early navigators found reflected the technology of their times. We may regard their instruments as crude, but their very simplicity means that workable versions producing acceptable results can be put together from the odds and ends found on most yachts.

Different early cultures, separated by time and geography, all mastered the science of navigation. They did not rely on celestial benevolence, a sixth sense, charms, incantations, or sacrifices, human or otherwise, but skills and knowledge based on the close observation of natural phenomena, the meticulous construction of mental maps, simple instruments, and detailed sailing directions.

All in the mind

Landmark Navigation

Route Navigation

Map Navigators

Land Mark Navigation

Wayfinding uses the map in your head; the starting point is navigating by landmarks. This is the basis of all exploration. You move out in one direction from a known base, noting distinctive features along the way, and then return using these landmarks. A known journey can be extended by going further, but if we wish to explore in a new direction we start out all over again from our base (see Figure 4.1). We all do it when we use landmark navigation to find our way back to our hotel in a strange city.

Route Navigation

Landmark navigation creates routes taking travellers from A to B. Routes are journeys made for a reason, whether it is to go to work, fetch water, to hunt, or trade. Remove its function and a route becomes history. The cattle trails of the American west are a good example.

Each route stands alone, illustrated in Figure 4.2. A route navigator knows the way from home to work and the route from home to the shopping centre, but to pick up a can of beans coming back from work he might have to return home before he can find the shopping centre.

In unknown regions, route navigators resort to landmark navigation to be sure of their way back to known territory.

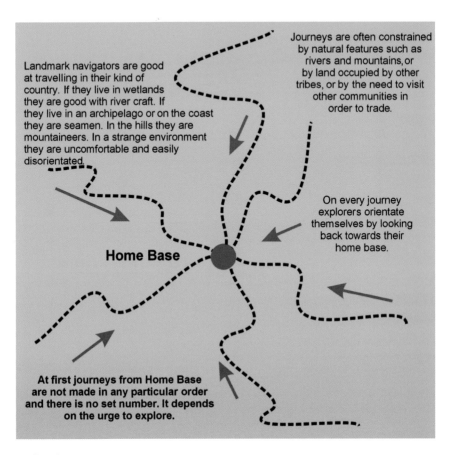

Landmark navigators are good at travelling in their kind of country. If they live in wetlands they are good with river craft. If they live in an archipelago or on the coast they are seamen. In the hills they are mountaineers. In a strange environment they are uncomfortable and easily disorientated.

Journeys are often constrained by natural features such as rivers and mountains, or by land occupied by other tribes, or by the need to visit other communities in order to trade.

Home Base

On every journey explorers orientate themselves by looking back towards their home base.

At first journeys from Home Base are not made in any particular order and there is no set number. It depends on the urge to explore.

4.1 Landmark Navigation

Map Navigators

Map navigators see the world around them as a whole. Their base is still used for finding direction and describing position but they also see features in relation to each other and frequently use a feature or the sun, stars, or the wind to orient themselves, even though their mental map remains orientated to their base. If they look at the midday sun and say 'There's north,' this is immediately followed by 'and that's the way

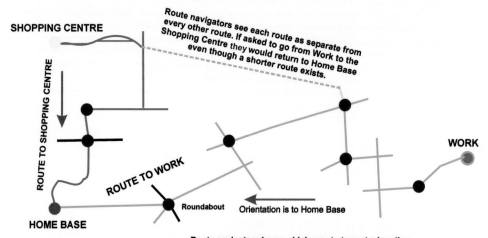

SHOPPING CENTRE

ROUTE TO SHOPPING CENTRE

Route navigators see each route as separate from every other route. If asked to go from Work to the Shopping Centre they would return to Home Base even though a shorter route exists.

ROUTE TO WORK

WORK

Roundabout

Orientation is to Home Base

HOME BASE

Route navigators know which way to turn at a junction and which exit to take at roundabouts but as far as they are concerned every other road at a junction is a dead end.

4.2 Route Navigation

home.' Compare this to navigating by map and compass, where you always orientate the map, and yourself, to north.

Map navigators can change routes to include intermediate destinations or make diversions if it is not possible to follow their chosen route (see Figure 4.3).

In areas they do not know, map navigators head in the general direction of their destination. If it lies to the west, they head westwards until they are close to their destination. Then they close in, either through recognising features around their destination or asking their way, a navigational trick my grandmother described as 'using your guid Scottish tongue'.

The Polynesians used islands along their route to confirm that they were on course. They called this Etak. More often than not the Etak island was out of sight over the horizon, as shown in Figure 4.4. Instead they looked for the zenith stars (see Chapter 16) that marked the Etak island and used these stars to judge the island's position and where they were in relation to it. Knowing which islands to use as Etaks, together with their zenith stars, was an important part of plotting their sailing routes.

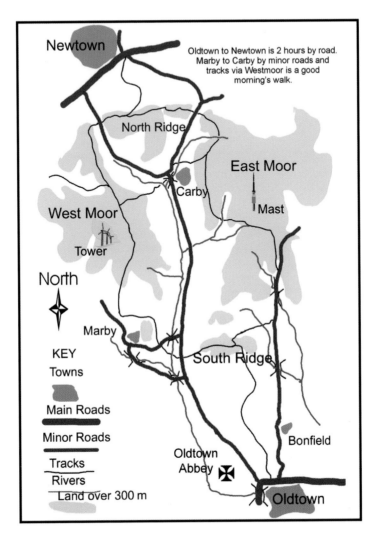

Oldtown to Newtown is 2 hours by road. Marby to Carby by minor roads and tracks via Westmoor is a good morning's walk.

4.3 Map Navigation. Map navigators carry mental maps of entire areas from which they can put together routes as they are needed. The scale of a mental map reflects its use. This map takes an overview but a map navigator can zoom in to a street map of Newtown or a floor plan of the Abbey. If you sketch a mental map for others, try to use easily understood symbols. Drawing mental maps to scale is very difficult. Journey times are a better indicator.

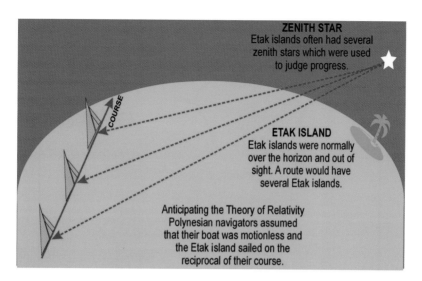

4.4 Etak Sailing

Etak navigation appears esoteric, but we use it without a second thought. I live in the North-east of England. On the other side of the hill is the town of Sunniside, shown in Figure 4.5. I cannot see it but I know that it is just to the right of the tall radio mast. Now that the mast has told me where Sunniside is I can fit other towns and villages over the horizon into my mental map.

The radio mast plays the role of an Etak star and Sunniside the Etak island. As long as the mast remains in sight I can check my progress. With luck, when I lose sight of it some other feature will play the same role. Without radio masts breaking their horizon the Polynesians used zenith stars.

Landmark, route and map navigation are not mutually exclusive skills. A good navigator switches from one to the other as circumstances require.

Scale

Charts bought in shops use a scale shown as a ratio such as 1:50,000, which means that one inch, centimetre or whatever on the map, represents 50,000 of the same units on the ground.

4.5 Landmarks as Etak Stars

Scale on mental maps does not use ratios or inches to the mile. A mental map looks nothing like a professionally drawn map, regardless of how well you know the area or your artwork:

1. Short complicated routes with many changes of direction occupy more space than long routes, with few changes of direction.

2. Familiar journeys contain more detail and occupy more space than rarely travelled routes.

3. The perception of time en route is more important than actual time and distance. A voyage that takes two days should occupy more space than a trip of one day, but a two-day familiar journey is often seen as quicker and it occupies less space.

These factors stretch your map here and squash it there, but with a little explanation the end result is understandable to others. The Polynesian's bamboo, shell, and pebble charts look confusing, but they were representations of mental maps drawn to pass information on to others. Soldiers do the same when they lay out items of equipment, stones, and twigs to represent the battlefield and use it to brief their troops.

Taking an Overview

Chart plotters tell you where you are without the effort of building up a mental map, but it is difficult to gain from them a detailed overview of your route or your relationship to other features. If you zoom in and scroll around, then how far have you scrolled and where are you in relation to your position, or your destination, or a danger? Zoom out to check, and detail disappears.

Passage planning

Choice of Landfall

One Step at a Time

Sailing Directions

Log Keeping

Navigating without instruments is a last resort. Plan A has sunk and Plan B leaks like a sieve. It is a time of great stress, so before beginning your passage without electronic instruments, prepare a new passage plan, as shown in Figure 5.1 Only implement this plan if you believe the odds on making a successful landfall are favourable. If not, then consider any other options open to you. It may be Hobson's choice. Even so, think long and hard before you go ahead.

Crash Bag Navigation is more than the mechanics of navigation. It includes gaining the confidence of your crew, drawing upon their skills, playing to their strengths, maximising their morale, confidence and enthusiasm, and keeping open the greatest number of options for the longest period of time.

Choice of Landfall

Once departures and landfalls, although still in sight of land, were some distance offshore. In making a departure, after a final solid fix using charted features the information to plot position diminishes in quality and quantity. A good astro-fix means a small circle of error. A few overcast days or some heavy weather creates one miles in diameter which is likely to be the position nearing land.

Similarly when approaching land, get a firm fix as early as possible (see Figure 5.2). Landfalls are dangerous. Your last reliable position may be several days and hundreds of miles astern. You could be entering tidal waters uncertain of the set and drift. Visibility may be less than good and the weather less than kind.

Serial	Action
1	Put the kettle on. Make and drink a cup of tea.
2	Review all the resources available to you. Are there charts, a magnetic compass, reliable watch, sextant, tables and almanac aboard? Have you the materials to make 1 A compass 2 A traverse board 3 A nocturnal 4 A sundial 5 A ship log 6 A homemade sextant 7 A plotting sheet. 8 Are there traverse tables on board or a calculator that will let you traverse sail? You may not need all of these items but the longer you expect to be at sea the more of them you will require.
3	Discuss the situation with the crew. Hear what they have to say. Draw upon their expertise and experience and listen to their suggestions.
4	Prepare a list of possible destinations. See Table 5.2 for the criteria to take into account when choosing a destination.
5	Choose what you consider the best destination. You may well decide to continue towards your original destination but this should be an informed decision and not the outcome of not knowing what else to do.
6	Prepare a detailed passage plan, just as you would for any other passage, drawing upon the information in any pilots on board and personal knowledge.
7	Outline the position to the crew. Put them fully in the picture.
8	Tell the crew your plan. Explain your decisions and the reasoning.
9	Brief the crew on how you intend to execute your plan, making sure each crew member understands the role they will play.

5.1 Beginning Crash Bag Sailing – initial actions

In these circumstances forget pinpoint landfalls and select the biggest, most obvious landfall you can find. Aim for a general area rather than a specific point and make a landfall covering as wide an area across your course as possible.

Serial	Topic	Remarks
1	Distance to landfall	1. If you know only the latitude and longitude of alternative destinations then without a chart you will need traverse tables to calculate the course and distance. 2. The distance to your landfall is not the straight line distance. You may need to put in a dog leg to avoid hazards or make a favourable approach to your landfall. 3. If you are latitude sailing then you will have to sail north or south until you are on the latitude of your destination and then sail east or west along that latitude until you arrive. 4. If you are aiming for an island group lay courses to maximise the size of the island group. Sailing from the Marquesas towards Hawaii you are aiming along the Hawaiian chain and have a fairly narrow target. It is best to sail north until the Hawaiian islands, bear west and then alter course to hit the chain broadside on.
2	Hazards en route	1. Are there any hazards such as reefs or banks en route? If so, how easy is it to be sure of missing them?
3	Expected time on passage	1. Downwind sailing is faster than upwind beating. If your closest landfall is upwind it may not be the nearest in time. 2. If the choice is equally balanced between a port one day's sail away and another a week's sail away, then pick the port a day's sail away even if the other port was your original destination.
4	Expected weather	1. This will be based on the forecasts you had before losing the instruments. You did keep a record of what the Navtex said?

5	Type of landfall	1. Is your landfall
		  a. A low solitary island? If so your navigation must be of the highest quality and accurate to within a handful of miles.
		  b. A high solitary island? Better than a low island. Accuracy is now measured in tens of miles.
		  c. An island chain? Accuracy can now be in hundreds of miles.

5.2 Choosing a Landfall

		d. A featureless coastline? Difficult to miss but aim off so that you know which way to turn when you arrive. e. A headland? f. A river estuary? Often can only be entered on the flood. Often have bars. Can be dangerous in some conditions. 2. What hazards are there around your landfall? 3. How far away will you be when you pick up your landfall? Obviously the further off, the better. 4. Once you have picked up your landfall how easy will it be to get a fix? 5. How far offshore will you be when you get your fix?
6	Can you safely arrive upwind and up current of your landfall?	1. This has many advantages and is especially important if your landfall is an island. After a long arduous passage it will be hard, physically and mentally, on everyone on board to beat up to your destination knowing that any error may see you swept past it and out to sea. 2. If your landfall is on a long coastline it is unlikely that you will make a pinpoint landfall. Far better to aim off so that when land is reached you know which way to turn to reach your destination.
7	The strengths and weaknesses of the crew (and yourself)	1. Only you know the answer this question and the effect your answer will have on your decision. This includes not only physical and technical skills but morale and attitude of mind. If people believe failure is inevitable the odds on failing are very high. Before Louis Bombard sailed his inflatable L'Hérétique across the Atlantic without food or water he had discovered that during WW2 many torpedoed crews in lifeboats believed they would die and did, even though conditions were such they should have survived. Bombard wanted to prove his point and he did: a great, bold voyage. You and your crew must truly believe that you can reach your landfall.

5.2 (Continued)

Horta on the island of Fayal in the Azores is a favourite watering hole for yachts returning to Europe from the Caribbean. Fayal is a small island but it is one of four in a 50-mile area of sea, the lowest of which is visible from 30 miles away. Immediately beyond Fayal is Isla Pico with Portugal's highest point, Mt Pico – 2351 metres, (7713 feet). On a clear day this is visible from 100 miles away, more if it is covered in a cap of cloud. Your landfall is now 200 miles wide and has a bullseye leading you straight into Horta and Cafe Sport. However, any island in the group will give you a fix and point you towards Horta (as shown in Figure 5.3).

The arc of Caribbean islands from St Martin in the north to Grenada in the south is almost 400 miles long. Each island is visible from 25 to 30 miles offshore, perhaps more. The distance between each pair of islands is 40 miles or less. For a vessel

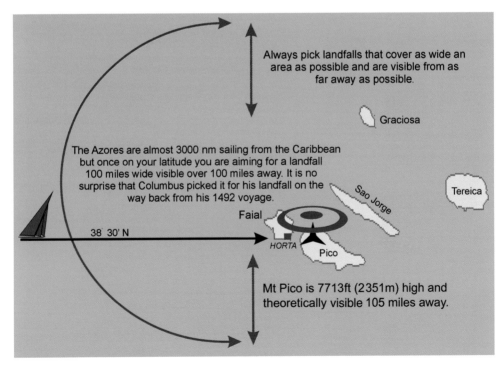

5.3 Island Group Landfall

approaching from the east it adds up to a landfall covering nearly 400 miles. You may not land on your chosen island but you would arrive in the Caribbean.

Always arrange your course so that your landfall is at right angles to a line of islands. This is especially important approaching a chain of low lying islands. When closing at right angles to their long axis the odds are that you are likely to see one of them. From any other direction, being off track by a few miles could mean missing them all, as demonstrated in Figure 5.4.

Always select a landfall easily identifiable from a long way off. Waypoints that bring cliffy headlands broadside on are good, as in Figure 5.5. Normally the headland is seen long before you reach your landfall and you can immediately begin redefining your position. Once at your landfall waypoint you will have enough information to make a good fix and sail to your (pinpoint) destination.

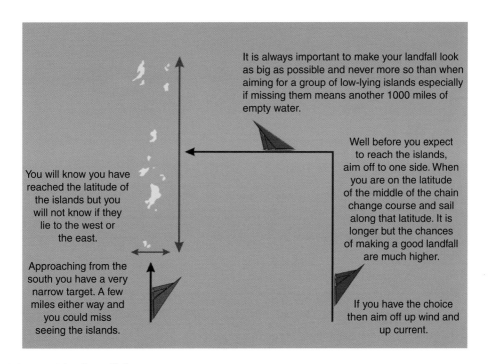

It is always important to make your landfall look as big as possible and never more so than when aiming for a group of low-lying islands especially if missing them means another 1000 miles of empty water.

You will know you have reached the latitude of the islands but you will not know if they lie to the west or the east.

Well before you expect to reach the islands, aim off to one side. When you are on the latitude of the middle of the chain change course and sail along that latitude. It is longer but the chances of making a good landfall are much higher.

Approaching from the south you have a very narrow target. A few miles either way and you could miss seeing the islands.

If you have the choice then aim off up wind and up current.

5.4 Low Island Landfall

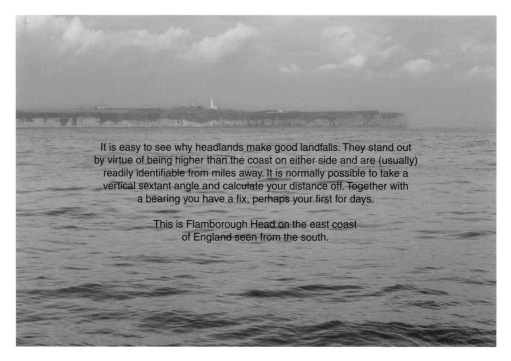

It is easy to see why headlands make good landfalls. They stand out by virtue of being higher than the coast on either side and are (usually) readily identifiable from miles away. It is normally possible to take a vertical sextant angle and calculate your distance off. Together with a bearing you have a fix, perhaps your first for days.

This is Flamborough Head on the east coast of England seen from the south.

5.5 Headland Landfall

Deliberate Error

Direct reckoning (DR) positions are almost certainly wrong, but *how* wrong? When approaching a featureless coast, or a hazard such as a reef, introduce an error of your own choosing and steer a course which avoids the danger, or tells you which way to turn when you sight land.

The Dutch coastline is mostly featureless dyke. Sailing from Lowestoft or Harwich towards Ijmuiden you could be almost anywhere, until you spot the harbour piers. Select a landfall a few miles south or north, so that when you see land you know which way to turn to reach Ijmuiden (as shown in Figure 5.6). Aim off rather more than your maximum expected error. If you expect to be 10 miles off course when you reach land, then aim off 11 miles.

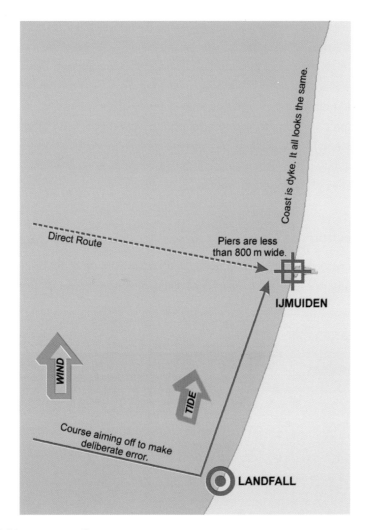

5.6 Landfall by Aiming Off

One Step at a Time

Break routes into as many legs as possible, the more the better. If possible, arrange that each leg ends with a fix from which you can start a new plot. This way you make a series of short passages, each starting from a known position.

It is 90 miles from Zeebrugge in Belgium to Lowestoft, but it is possible to plot a route where the gaps between buoys are mostly 10 miles or less. The longest leg is 20 miles and that is on the run in to a landfall between Southwold and Benacre Ness where an error of a mile or so is not critical (see Figure 5.7). What at first looks like a long, demanding offshore passage becomes a series of short hops, each starting from a known position and bringing you to a recognisable landfall south of your destination. Completing each leg successfully is a cause for celebration, a boost to your confidence. A passage that may overwhelm your confidence when seen as a whole, can be broken down into a series of manageable chunks.

Sailing Directions

Sailors always recorded sailing directions. In societies with an oral tradition, navigators underwent a long apprenticeship learning sailing directions by heart. Sometimes this

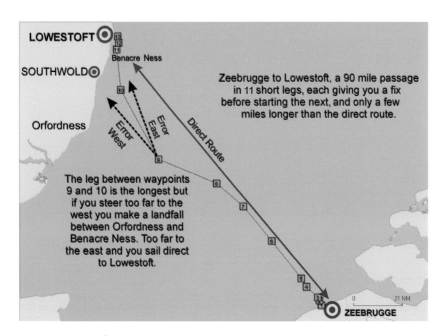

5.7 Point to Point Sailing

seemed similar to preparation for the priesthood, as navigators were seen as possessing skills beyond human ken.

Even with the latest navigational aid, entering a strange port for the first time is never as easy as entering a familiar harbour. If you have a choice, go for a destination you know,whose features are burned into your mind. If you must enter a strange harbour then gather as much information about it as possible and plan to enter in daylight with a favourable tide.

Log Keeping

In the past, details of course and distance were kept on a traverse board – check out Figure 5.8. These were used well into the 19th century. If paper and pencil are scarce

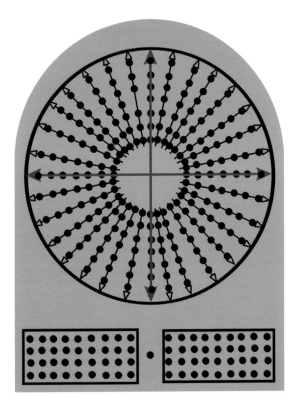

5.8 A traverse board. See Chapter 11 on how to use a traverse board. The one shown uses the traditional 32 point compass. If you want to work in degrees then use 36 rows of holes, each row representing 10 degrees

this may still be a useful way to record speed and course changes during a watch, but it is also necessary to keep track of other changes in your local environment. The early navigators probably did so instinctively and would have been surprised at our lack of innate awareness. Encourage everyone to watch for changes in the waves, swells, winds, the sky, the temperature, and the presence and behaviour of seabirds that may warn you of a wind shift, approaching bad weather, or land. Note these down. Write up the log at least once every watch, on every change of course. Note if there is any change in wind or sea conditions, and when a DR or EP is worked up.

Life Goes On

While you are Crash Bag Navigating, keep to the usual ship's routine of watch-keeping and housekeeping duties. Normality boosts confidence.

A home-made magnetic compass

The Compass Rose

Making a Magnetic Compass

The Compass Rose

For centuries sailors found direction by the wind and often named winds by destination. Pliny wrote of sailing the 50 miles from 'Carpathus to Rhodes with Africus', Africus being the wind. The four cardinal winds were divided into 32 half and quarter winds, giving a course to within one point (11.25°). In the early 13th century, wind roses appeared on Portolan charts, with rhumb lines springing from wind roses in the centre, or around the edge of the chart.

Using winds for naming direction is fine if they are constant. Frisian navigators in North Europe, where wind direction varies hourly, called the cardinal points Nord, Ost, Sud and West and used compounds of these words for the intermediate compass points, creating the system we use today.

Making a Magnetic Compass

With the materials found on most boats, it is possible to magnetise a needle and float it on a dish of water to discover magnetic north (see Figures 6.1 to 6.3.)

If you feel that one needle is not enough to swing the straw then use two or three needles. Be sure that all the north poles point in the same direction (see Figure 6.4).

A fair estimate of variation can be found by pointing the bows at Polaris and noting where the compass needle points, or by holding a thin wooden or plastic rod, thinner than a pencil, over the compass needle at local noon. The angle made by the shadow of the rod and the compass needle is, approximately, the magnetic variation.

Serial	Item
1	One needle, a very small nail, a straightened out paper clip or similar.
2	One magnet or a silk cloth. Magnets are found in stereo speakers.
3	One plastic bowl, traditionally round but any shape will do. A Tupperware type bowl is good, so is cutting out a plastic bottle to make a bowl. If a plastic bowl is not available use any small non-ferrous bowl.
4	Water or light oil.
5	Two tiny pieces of cork or a drinking straw or a couple of fragments of polystyrene foam. Tradition has it that in the early compasses the needle was pushed through a straw to form a cross.
6	Some cling film if you have it. This is to cover the bowl and stop the water or oil slopping about. If you have no cling film use water rather than oil.

6.1   Magnetic Compass Component List

Serial	Action
1	Hold the needle in one hand and the magnet in the other.
2	Put the north end of the needle in the middle of the magnet and draw it along the needle towards the point. If you do not know which end of the magnet is north then make a guess. See Figure 6.3
3	Repeat this about 20 or so times.
4	Turn the magnet over and draw from the middle of the needle towards the eye of the needle about 20 times.
5	If you have no magnet then rub the needle vigorously on a silk cloth or in your hair for a couple of minutes.
6	Using either method, by the time you have stopped rubbing you have magnetized the needle and it behaves just like a compass needle. The magnetism diminishes with time and you will need to stroke the needle every few days.
7	Stick a tiny piece of cork, polystyrene foam, straw, or anything light that floats on each end of the needle so it floats.
8	Fill the bowl with oil or water. Use seawater if water is scarce.
9	Place the needle on the water or oil in a small bowl.
10	Wrap a layer of cling film over the bowl to protect it from the wind. The water or oil acts as natural gimbals.

6.2   Making a Magnetic Compass

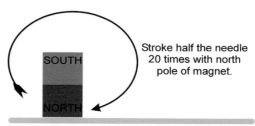

Stroke half the needle 20 times with north pole of magnet.

SOUTH

NORTH

Needle, paper clip or any thin iron wire

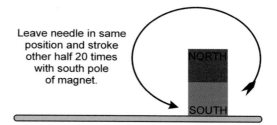

Leave needle in same position and stroke other half 20 times with south pole of magnet.

NORTH

SOUTH

6.3 Magnetizing a Needle

Any non-ferrous container will serve as a compass bowl for your magnetised needles. This is the plastic cap from a jar of instant coffee. The needles are supported by a short length of plastic drinking straw. The water acts as natural gimbals. If you are using more than one needle it is best to use an even number of needles. Try to space them evenly along the straw.

6.4 A Homemade Magnetic Compass

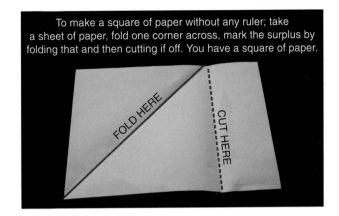

To make a square of paper without any ruler; take a sheet of paper, fold one corner across, mark the surplus by folding that and then cutting if off. You have a square of paper.

FOLD HERE

CUT HERE

6.5 Making a Paper Square

You can also check your compass error against an amplitude, (see Chapter 7). Minimise deviation by keeping your compass away from anything that may influence it.

A Home-Made Compass Card

The compass rose cut out from a chart makes a compass card. Tape it to a board, extend its radii and place it under your compass bowl.

If you do not have a spare compass rose, or a protractor to draw one, fold a square of paper (see Figure 6.5 and Figure 6.5b), to get eight compass points. Insert

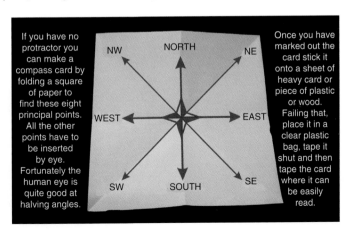

If you have no protractor you can make a compass card by folding a square of paper to find these eight principal points. All the other points have to be inserted by eye. Fortunately the human eye is quite good at halving angles.

NW   NORTH   NE

WEST   EAST

SW   SOUTH   SE

Once you have marked out the card stick it onto a sheet of heavy card or piece of plastic or wood. Failing that, place it in a clear plastic bag, tape it shut and then tape the card where it can be easily read.

6.5b A Homemade Compass Card

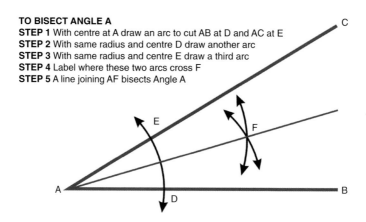

TO BISECT ANGLE A
STEP 1 With centre at A draw an arc to cut AB at D and AC at E
STEP 2 With same radius and centre D draw another arc
STEP 3 With same radius and centre E draw a third arc
STEP 4 Label where these two arcs cross F
STEP 5 A line joining AF bisects Angle A

6.5c Bisecting Any Angle

the rest by eye or by geometrically bisecting the angles as in Figure 6.5c. When you have all 32 points, label them, see Figure 6.6.

If you wish to work in degrees then draw a circle with a radius of 57 units. The units can be any you wish: millimetres, tenths of an inch, or the thickness of a couple of coins taped together, see Figure 6.7. The circumference of a circle with a radius of 57 units is almost exactly 360 of the same units and one unit around the circumference represents 1°.

6.6 Traditional 32 Point Compass Card

The edges of these one dollar coins are as near as makes no difference 2mm thick. If you have no ruler coins are a useful way of measuring small distances. Check your change before you sail.

2mm

6.7 Using Coins for Small Measurements

A home made floating compass is useless for taking bearings. For doubling the angle on the bow (see Chapter 12) you may wish to make a pelorous where the bow is 0° and the card is marked 0°–180° port and starboard. When you align the 0° –180° line along the centreline of the boat, all angles measured with this pelorous are relative (see Figure 6.8).

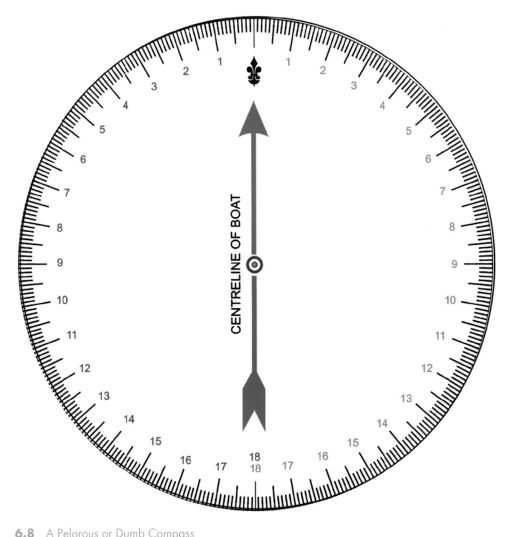

6.8 A Pelorous or Dumb Compass

Direction from the sun

Amplitudes

North by Your Watch

A Sun Compass

At local noon the sun makes its meridian passage. It then bears due south in the northern hemisphere and due north in the southern hemisphere. Once you have found true north at local noon then it is straightforward to insert the other cardinal and inter-cardinal points around your horizon and then for the rest of the day the sun acts as a check against direction, see Figure 7.1.

Amplitudes

An amplitude is the bearing of a celestial body as it rises or sets, illustrated in Figure 7.2 and Figure 7. 2b. To calculate a body's amplitude you need to know

> 1. Its declination
>
> 2. Your latitude.

Lacking tables you need a calculator that can handle simple trigonometry. The general formula is:

$$Amplitude = sin^{-1} (sin\ declination\ of\ body/cos\ your\ latitude).$$

Even if the declination and your latitude have different names, ie, one is north and the other is south, all the figures are taken as positive. Once you have the answer you will need to convert it into a bearing as shown in Figures 7.3, 7.3b and 7.4.

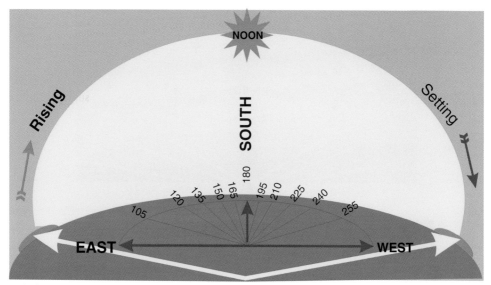

NOON

Rising

Setting

SOUTH

105 120 135 150 165 180 195 210 225 240 255

EAST

WEST

In the northern hemisphere when you face the noonday sun you are facing due south. In the southern hemisphere you are facing due north. It is straightforward to interpolate other cardinal points and bearings and to use the passage of the sun during the day to confirm your direction. It is rare for the sun to rise due east or set due west.

7.0 Facing South

Pinpoint accuracy is always best but approximations can give surprisingly good results. At exactly local noon in the northern hemisphere the sun is due south and a shadow from a vertical stick will point due north. On an amble in the hills I think it is about local noon. I'm not certain for I'm not sure of my longitude but I take my best guess and the compass shows I'm not far out, certainly close enough to steer a course. The shadow stick method is impossible at sea but you can always guess when the sun is on its zenith.

7.1 The Sun at Noon

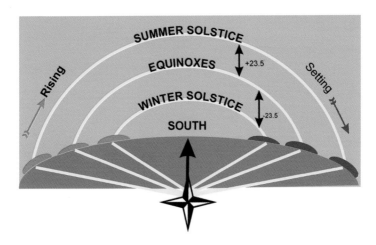

7.2 Seasonal Path of the Sun

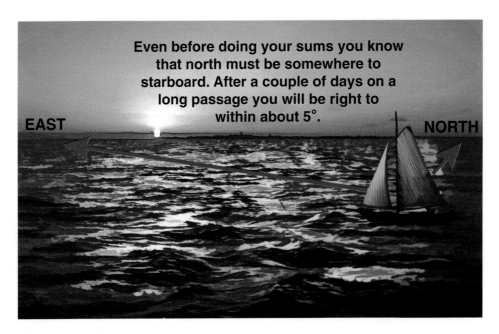

7.2b Amplitude by Rising Sun

An amplitude is taken when a celestial body is exactly on the horizon. Imagine you are watching the sun rise at 41°N and the sun's declination is 23.5°N.

$$Amplitude = sin^{-1}(sin\ 23.5\ divided\ by\ cos\ 41)$$
$$= sin^{-1}(0.3987\ divided\ by\ 0.7547)$$
$$= sin^{-1}(0.5283)$$
$$= 31.8899°$$

Call this 32°

Sin-1is calculator speak. What it means is that when you have finished dividing the sine of a body's declination by the cosine of your latitude then you hit the shift key on your calculator immediately followed by the sine key.

The exact keystrokes will vary from calculator to calculator. The shift key is sometimes called the mode key. Read the instructions to discover yours.

By the rules in Figure 7.4 the sun was rising so the amplitude is east.

The declination was north so the amplitude is north.

This translates your amplitude to a bearing of E32°N.

This is shorthand for saying the bearing was 32° north of east (Figure 7.3b). In 360 nomenclature east is 090° and 32° north from that is

$$90–32 = 058°$$

If the sun had been setting the bearing would have been W32°N (Figure 7.3b). In 360 nomenclature west is 270° so

$$W32°N = 270° + 32° = 302°$$

If the declination had been south then the bearing would have been W32°S and

$$W32°S = 270° – 32° = 238°$$

Laid out like this it all looks more complicated than it is in practice. If you do not have a compass then twice-a-day amplitudes of the sun will give you a known direction. Added to finding north at noon it adds up to three checks each day. If you have a compass then amplitudes are a useful means of checking its accuracy.

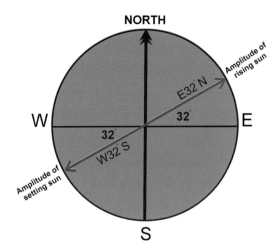

7.3 Amplitudes Worked Example

7.3b Amplitudes and Bearings

If you know the declination of several stars then you can check your direction throughout the night. On a practical note, the sun lets you know it is coming over the horizon. A rising star is halfway up the sky before you have noticed it. Setting stars are best for amplitudes.

There are four simple rules to follow to turn an amplitude into a bearing:

Serial	Rule
1	Amplitudes are east when the body is rising
2	Amplitudes are west when the body is setting
3	Amplitudes are north (of east or west) when the declination is north
4	Amplitudes are south when the declination is south.

7.4 Converting Amplitudes to Bearings

North by Your Watch

If you have a watch with hour and minute hands and you are between latitudes 35–55°, you can always find an approximation of north, as shown in Figures 7.5 and 7.5b.

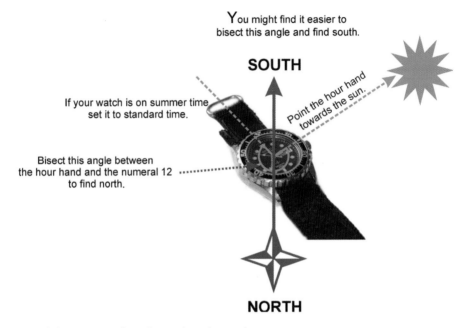

7.5 North by your watch in the northern hemisphere

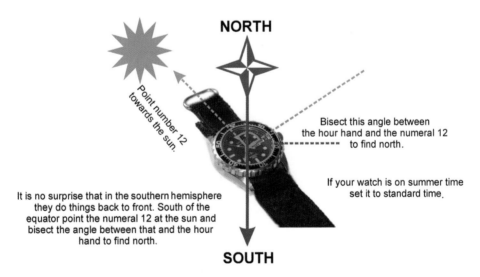

7.5b North by your watch in the southern hemisphere

A Sun Compass

How did the Vikings find their way? The sagas mention shore-sighting birds. Some argue that Vikings had the magnetic compass long before the rest of Europe. Others claim they used the stars, forgetting that in the long days of the Norse cruising season, sunlight blots out the stars. Perhaps they used a sunstone to polarise sunlight and find their direction even when the sky was overcast, but it is more likely that, when overcast, the shadow thrown by a knife blade gave direction, see Figure 7.6.

In the early 1990s part of a 7cm wooden disk was found on an archaeological dig of Viking ruins in Uunartoq Fjord, Greenland, which has been identified as a form of sun compass.

A sun compass is an analemmatic sundial used to find direction rather than time. For crossing deserts in tanks and trucks sun compasses had a niche market until the introduction of GPS. A magnetic compass is useless in a vehicle unless the vehicle stops and the navigator walks away from it. Commercial sun compasses are set up for

**FINDING THE DIRECTION OF THE SUN
WHEN THE SKY IS OVERCAST**
1. Hold knife over a light coloured surface.
2. Rotate knife slowly, watching the shadow it casts.
3. When shadow is thinnest the reciprocal of its
   shadow is the direction of the sun.

This will not work if the cloud cover is too thick, and at best, the shadow will be fuzzy, rather than a crisp, clear line.

7.6 Using Shadows to find the Direction of the Sun

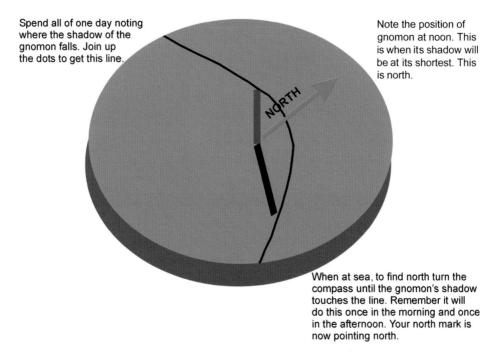

Spend all of one day noting where the shadow of the gnomon falls. Join up the dots to get this line.

NORTH

Note the position of gnomon at noon. This is when its shadow will be at its shortest. This is north.

When at sea, to find north turn the compass until the gnomon's shadow touches the line. Remember it will do this once in the morning and once in the afternoon. Your north mark is now pointing north.

7.6b A Sun Compass

different latitudes and different times of the year, but you can make a one-time Viking sun compass.

Before you set sail, take a piece of wood – circular looks best, square is fine. Fit a short gnomon in the centre. Place it in a suitably sunny spot, level it off, and spend one day marking the tip of the sun's shadow on the board at half-hourly intervals. At the end of the day, join the dots into a curved line. The shortest shadow is noon and this points north. Draw in the other compass points. You have a sun compass, see Figure 7.6b.

To find north during the day hold the board level and turn it until the sun's shadow touches the line. The north you drew now points north. There are serious limitations. The sun's shadow changes with its declination, so this sun compass is only good for a couple of weeks. Secondly it is, at most, accurate over a couple of degrees of latitude.

Direction from the stars

The Celestial Sphere

Finding Polaris

Meridian Stars

Planets

The Celestial Sphere

Most modern mariners are unfamiliar with the night sky. The stars are strangers and we become lost amongst the spinning celestial maze.

Think of the earth at the centre of a great sphere, with the stars and planets stuck on the inside (see Figure 8.1). We can only see half of this sphere so imagine a flat world with the sky as a great dome above our heads. Where the dome meets the earth is our horizon and our zenith is directly above our heads, shown in Figure 8.2.

The earth's rotation makes it look like the stars, planets, sun, and moon rise in the east, move across the sky and set in the west.

The only exceptions are stars near the north and south poles. These remain above the horizon and circle the pole. Their number varies with latitude: the higher your latitude, the more circumpolar the stars.

Celestial Coordinates

Just like the earth, the celestial sphere has its system of coordinates that define position.

The north–south position of anything on the celestial sphere is called its declination, but as the North and South Celestial Poles are directly above the earth's poles and the celestial equator parallels the earth's equator, (see Figure 8.1) the declination of any celestial body is the same as its latitude if it were on earth, (see Figure 8.3).

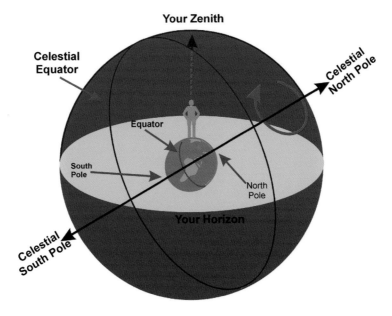

8.1 The Celestial Sphere from Space

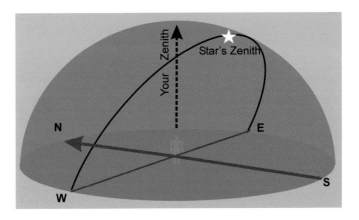

8.2 The Observer's Celestial Sphere

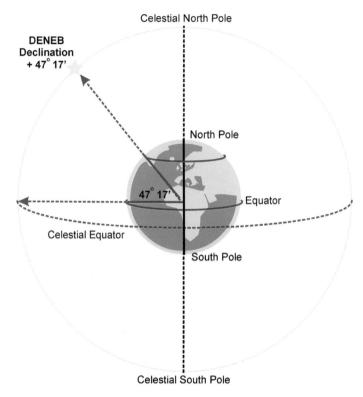

8.3 Declination of a Celestial Body

The starting point for measuring the sun's east–west position on the Celestial Sphere is the Greenwich meridian and since time and arc can be swapped back and forth, we talk of Greenwich Hour Angles. This neatly combines time and arc to remind you that, with a little arithmetic, they are interchangeable.

The stars have their version of the Greenwich Meridian. The ecliptic is the path the earth takes as it orbits the sun. This cuts the celestial equator at equinoxes. Where the sun crosses the ecliptic at the spring (or vernal) equinox is called the First Point of Aries and is the equivalent of the Greenwich meridian for stars (see Figure 8.4). A star's east–west coordinates are called its Sidereal Hour Angle (SHA) and are measured westwards from the First Point of Aries. SHA can be thought of as a celestial body's

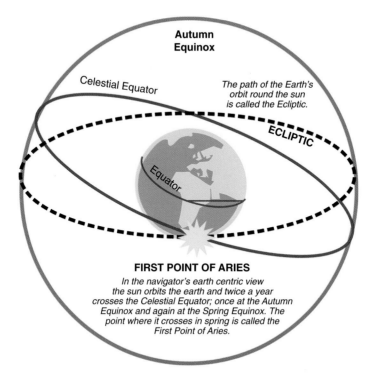

8.4 The Ecliptic

longitude. Do not take this analogy too far. The First Point of Aries does not correspond to the position of the Greenwich meridian on earth.

Altitude and Azimuth

The height of a celestial body above the horizon is called its altitude. Do not confuse altitude with declination. A star's declination is constant. Altitude varies during the course of the day unless you are looking at the Pole star.

The bearing of a celestial body from true north is called its azimuth (shown in Figure 8.5).

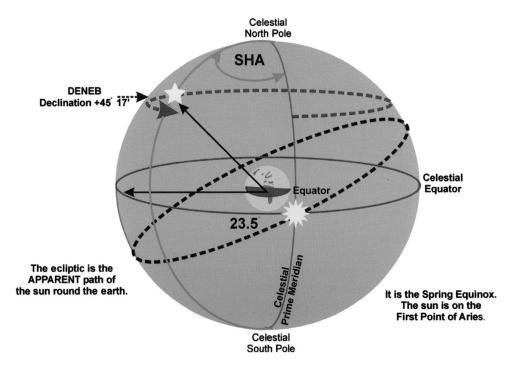

Celestial
North Pole

SHA

DENEB
Declination +45° 17″

Celestial
Equator

Equator

23.5°

The ecliptic is the
APPARENT path of
the sun round the earth.

Celestial
Prime Meridian

It is the Spring Equinox.
The sun is on the
First Point of Aries.

Celestial
South Pole

8.4b Sidereal Hour Angle

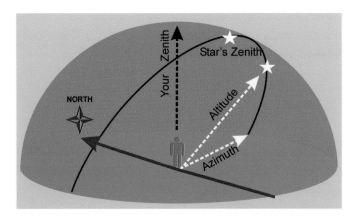

Your Zenith

Star's Zenith

NORTH

Altitude

Azimuth

8.5 A Star's Azimuth

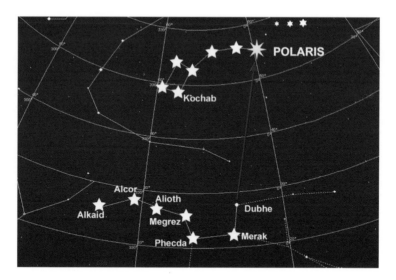

8.6 Polaris from the Big Dipper

Finding Polaris

To find Polaris, look for the Big Dipper and find the Dipper's ladle. Extend the line joining the two stars that make up the ladle across the sky for a distance equivalent to five times the depth of the ladle and you have Polaris (Figure 8.6). When you face Polaris you are facing true north.

If Polaris is obscured, but you can see the Big Dipper and its Pointers, then hold a stick at arm's length and mark on it the distance between the Pointers. Mark this distance off five times from the tip of the stick. Hold the marked stick at arm's length, parallel to the Pointers and the first of your marks on Dubhe. The tip of your stick is now on Polaris (see Figure 8.7).

North from Polaris

Right now Polaris is less than 1° from the true pole and circles the Pole every 24 hours. Anything that points north to within one degree is fine for helming, but you will need to find the true pole if you are using Polaris for latitude, (see Chapter 16).

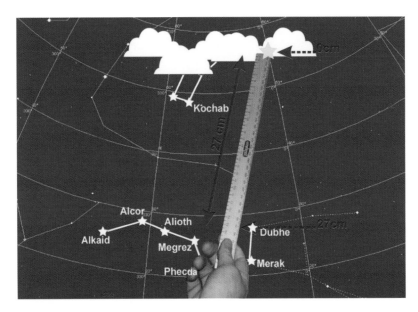

8.7 Finding Polaris in a Cloudy Sky

Precession of the Equinoxes

Because the earth's axis wobbles, Polaris has not always pointed north. Project this wobble out into space and every 28 500 years it makes one revolution. Stars on or very close to the circumference of this circle take their turn at being the north star. In 8000 years time it will be Deneb's turn.

The earth's wobble also causes the First Point of Aries to slip along the ecliptic. This is called the precession of the equinoxes (shown in Figure 8.8). Since SHA is measured from the First Point of Aries, star declinations also change and every 25 years, star atlases are redrawn.

North from Cassiopeia

The five stars making up Cassiopeia, on the opposite side of Polaris, look like the letter W. A line from the middle of the W brings you to Polaris, (see Figure 8.9 and Figure 8.9b).

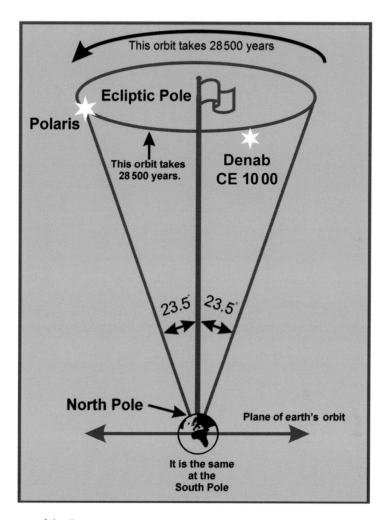

This orbit takes 28 500 years

Ecliptic Pole

Polaris

This orbit takes
28 500 years.

**Denab
CE 10 00**

23.5° 23.5°

North Pole

Plane of earth's orbit

It is the same
at the
South Pole

8.8 Precession of the Equinoxes

North from Pegasus

Pegasus looks like a bigger version of the Big Dipper and the two stars in its dipper (the Great Square Pegasus) lead to Polaris in the same way as the Pointers, and with the same ratio distance (1:5) between stars and Polaris (shown in Figure 8.10).

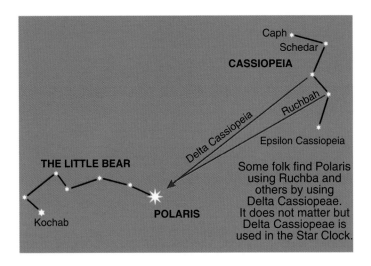

8.9 Polaris from Cassiopeia

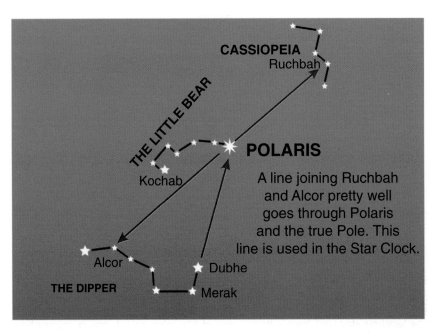

8.9b Polaris from Cassiopeia and the Dipper

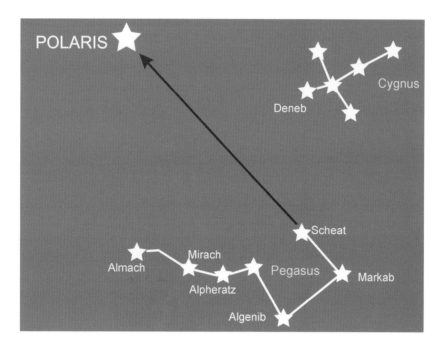

8.10 Polaris from Pegasus

The Summer Triangle

The Summer Triangle (in Figure 8.11) is not an official constellation but made up by the bluish white Deneb (apparent magnitude 1.26) in the tail of Cygnus the Swan; the yellow-white Altair (apparent magnitude 0.77) in Aquila the Eagle, and bluish Vega (apparent magnitude 0.04) in Lyra. These are bright, obvious stars. Vega is the second brightest star in the northern hemisphere.

Orion's Belt

From anywhere on earth Orion's Belt (see Figure 8.12) rises due east and sets due west. The leading star on Orion's Belt is called Mintaka, which has a declination of almost zero and circles the equator.

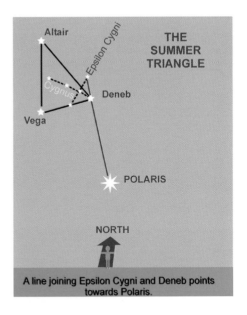

THE SUMMER TRIANGLE

Altair

Epsilon Cygni

Cygnus

Deneb

Vega

POLARIS

NORTH

A line joining Epsilon Cygni and Deneb points towards Polaris.

8.11 The Summer Triangle

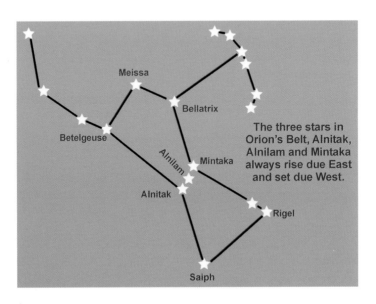

Meissa

Bellatrix

Betelgeuse

Alnilam

Mintaka

Alnitak

Rigel

Saiph

The three stars in Orion's Belt, Alnitak, Alnilam and Mintaka always rise due East and set due West.

8.12 Orion the Hunter

In the Southern Hemisphere

Using their myths and imaginations Greek and Arab astronomers gave picturesque names to stars and constellations. When western navigators reached the South Sea they ignored the names the Polynesians wove round their stars and gave the stars boring Latin names such as *Acrux* which is short for *Alpha Crux* instead of the Polynesians' more evocative *Ka Mole Honua* which means the *Foundation of the Earth.*

The southern hemisphere has no equivalent to Polaris and finding north from the stars is more difficult. Find the Southern Cross (shown in Figure 8.13) identify the long axis of the cross and extend it by drawing an imaginary line across the sky for five times the length of the long axis. You are now facing due south.

Meridian Stars

Like the sun the stars also make meridian passages and point the way to true north. You do not need to identify stars to do this, only be sure that they are at their zenith (see Figure 8.14).

Any two stars making their meridian transit at the same instant are in a north–south line. Meridian stars in the northern hemisphere point north, those in the southern hemisphere point south. You use this principle when the Southern Cross stands vertical and you follow the two stars (Gacrux on top and Acrux on the bottom) that make the upright of the Southern Cross to find due south.

A Star to Steer By

A sequence of stars of the same declination, whether or not they are zenith stars, will rise at the same point on the eastern horizon and set on the same point in the west. Once the boat is on course, find the stars rising on the bow, and use them to steer by. As one swings up across the sky and no longer points the way, another will rise to take its place (see Figure 8.15).

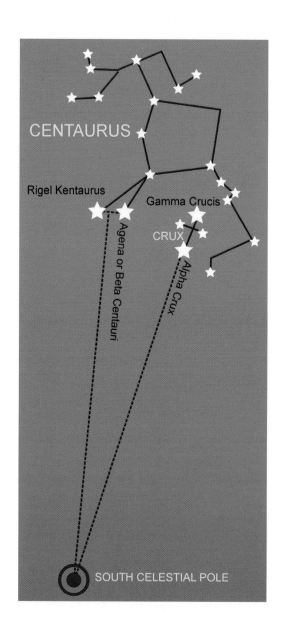

CENTAURUS

Rigel Kentaurus

Gamma Crucis

Agena or Beta Centauri

CRUX

Alpha Crux

SOUTH CELESTIAL POLE

8.13 The Southern Cross

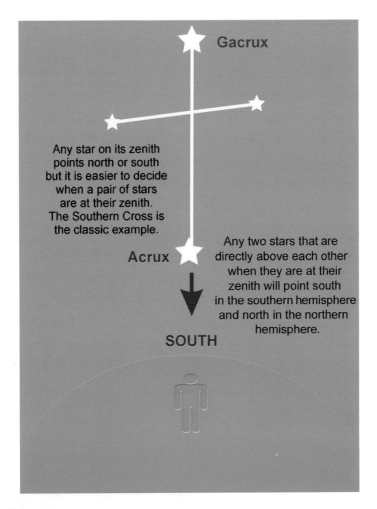

Gacrux

Any star on its zenith points north or south but it is easier to decide when a pair of stars are at their zenith. The Southern Cross is the classic example.

Acrux

Any two stars that are directly above each other when they are at their zenith will point south in the southern hemisphere and north in the northern hemisphere.

SOUTH

8.14 Zenith Stars

Close to the equator the stars rise almost vertically from the eastern horizon and individual stars can be used to hold your course for some time. The further you are from the equator, stars soar across the sky at ever shallower angles and the time they can be used as steering marks becomes shorter and shorter. In higher latitudes the cry 'Give me a star to steer by' soon becomes 'Give me another star to steer by.' (See Figure 8.16.)

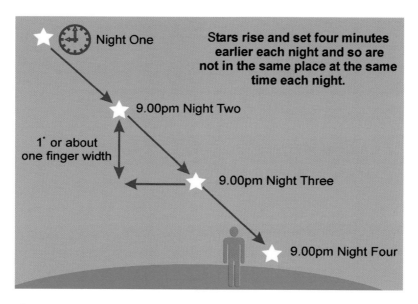

Stars rise and set four minutes earlier each night and so are not in the same place at the same time each night.

Night One

9.00pm Night Two

1° or about one finger width

9.00pm Night Three

9.00pm Night Four

8.15 Early Rising Stars

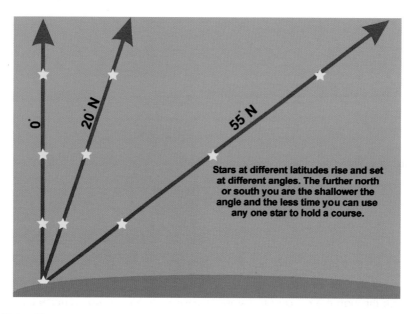

0°

20° N

55° N

Stars at different latitudes rise and set at different angles. The further north or south you are the shallower the angle and the less time you can use any one star to hold a course.

8.16 Rising Stars

If you are running down a parallel of latitude, then holding Polaris abeam keeps you sailing due east, or west.

Half-Latitude Rule

The half-latitude rule is another way of finding east or west. Stars with a northern declination will rise north of due east and set north of due west. Stars with a southern declination will rise south of due east and set south of due west.

When a star passes through your zenith it is at a height equal to your latitude and has moved away from due west or east by an angle equal to half your latitude. Outside the polar regions this is accurate to around five degrees. One advantage of the half-latitude rule is that you do not need to know which zenith stars you are using. Any will do.

Between about $10°$ north or south you can believe your zenith star rises off due east by an amount equal to its declination and sets off due west by the same amount. It is not true but works.

Apparent Magnitude

Apparent magnitude describes how bright a star appears. Sticking to the convention of the celestial sphere, apparent magnitude assumes all stars are the same distance away from the earth. Absolute magnitude is how bright a star really is and some of our dimmer stars are really very bright, but very distant, stars.

The brighter the star or planet the smaller the magnitude number. Some are so bright that they have negative magnitudes. Jupiter has a magnitude of between -2.1 to -2.6, Venus is -4.4 to -4.7 and the sun -27. The 6000 stars visible to the naked eye have a magnitude of 6.2 to 6. Not all are visible at the same time. On a good night you might see about 2000 stars with the naked eye.

When stars are low in the sky their light travels a long way through the earth's atmosphere. The scattering of their light by the atmosphere is at its greatest and they look quite dim (see Figure 8.17). As they travel higher in the sky their light takes a shorter path through the air and the stars appear brighter. Do not confuse this with a star's magnitude.

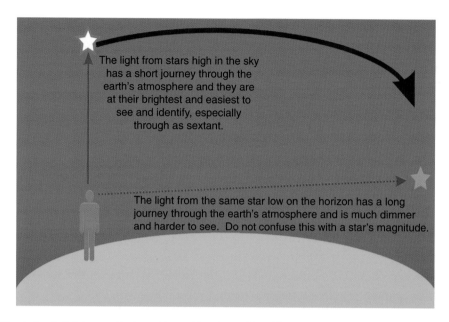

The light from stars high in the sky has a short journey through the earth's atmosphere and they are at their brightest and easiest to see and identify, especially through as sextant.

The light from the same star low on the horizon has a long journey through the earth's atmosphere and is much dimmer and harder to see. Do not confuse this with a star's magnitude.

8.17 A Star's Brightness Varies with its Altitude and Visiblity

Planets

Planets lie in a great arc across the sky with the sun and the moon and do not twinkle like stars. Not all planets are visible at the same time. Seen through moderately powered binoculars, they appear as small discs.

Jupiter and Venus are always much brighter than the stars, and a bright star seen occasionally near the morning or evening sun is as likely to be Mercury as Venus.

The Star Compass

The Polynesians developed a star compass. Look round your horizon and note the position where stars rise. These positions become your compass points. With luck you will be able to find a convoy of stars popping up one after the other at each compass point so that as one star climbs too high to use for direction, the next comes over the horizon.

Knowing the declination of stars we can produce a star compass in minutes. Take Betelgeuse, a bright star in the constellation of Orion. It has a declination of 7° N. From the equator, Betelgeuse rises on a bearing of 083°. Repeat this for stars around the horizon and you have your star compass where all bearings are true, and deviation or variation non-existent.

It sounds too good to be true. It is. For it works only as long as you stay within about 10° of the equator where the change in a star's bearing is only about six or seven degrees. Further north or south the bearing changes more quickly. Soon your star compass is useless. At higher latitudes you must make a new one every couple of degrees of latitude, and the increasing number of circumpolar stars means fewer stars to choose from.

Direction from the moon

The moon has no light of its own and the shape it takes as it reflects sunlight varies as it orbits the earth. When the moon is in the earth's shadow it reflects no, or very little, light. This is the time of the new moon. As the moon emerges from the earth's shadow, light reflects from its righthand side and grows, first into a crescent and then a full moon. Then it wanes, with the sunlight being reflected from its left side (see Figure 9.1).

The moon spends about half its life competing with the sun for prominence in the sky (see diagram in Figure 9.2). As a rule of thumb, if the moon rises before sunset, the illuminated side will be to the west. If it rises after midnight, the illuminated side will be towards the east.

If the moon is in one of its crescent phases, then a line joining the tips of the crescent down to the horizon will point approximately southwards in the northern hemisphere and northwards in the southern hemisphere (illustrated in Figure 9.3).

The moon rises about 50 minutes later each day, and from one new moon to the next is 29.5 days (one synodical month). A new moon occurs when the sun and moon are almost opposite each other, which is why a new moon rises around sunset and sets about sunrise.

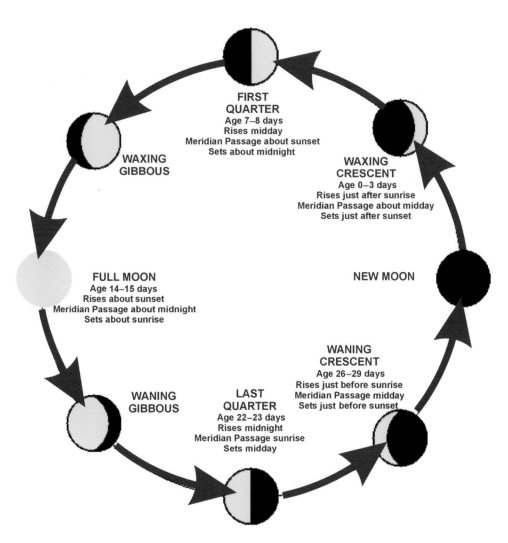

**FIRST
QUARTER**
Age 7–8 days
Rises midday
Meridian Passage about sunset
Sets about midnight

**WAXING
GIBBOUS**

**WAXING
CRESCENT**
Age 0–3 days
Rises just after sunrise
Meridian Passage about midday
Sets just after sunset

FULL MOON
Age 14–15 days
Rises about sunset
Meridian Passage about midnight
Sets about sunrise

NEW MOON

**WANING
CRESCENT**
Age 26–29 days
Rises just before sunrise
Meridian Passage midday
Sets just before sunset

**WANING
GIBBOUS**

**LAST
QUARTER**
Age 22–23 days
Rises midnight
Meridian Passage sunrise
Sets midday

Between new and full moons the moon is waxing and its lighted area is increasing.
From full to new moon the moon is waning and its lighted area is decreasing.
You can tell whether the moon is waxing or waning by whether the right side of the
moon is light or dark. In the southern hemisphere you decide whether or not the
left side is light or dark.

9.1   Phases of the Moon

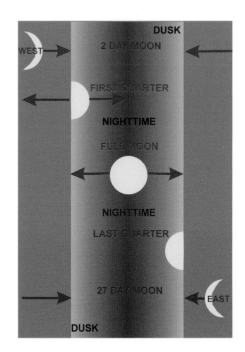

9.2 The Day Time Moon

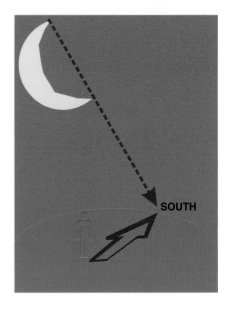

9.3 South from the Moon

Telling the time

GMT

As no meridian divides the globe into east and west in the same way as the equator divides the world into north and south, countries were free to pick their own. In 1675, Britain built the Royal Observatory and chose the Greenwich meridian. In 1880, after over 200 years of pick and mix, it was agreed Greenwich would be the universal Prime Meridian. In 1928 Universal time, shortened to UT1, became a synonym for GMT. Then in January 1972, Universal Coordinated Time, (UTC), using a worldwide selection of atomic clocks, was introduced.

GPS uses atomic time, which until January 1980 was the same as UTC. Since then leap seconds have been added to UTC (atomic time is more accurate and does not need these) resulting in nearly 15 seconds difference between GPS time and UTC. However, GPS makes its own corrections and the times it displays are within one second of UTC.

Zone Time

The world is divided into 24 time zones, each covering 15° of longitude. Zone Zero is 7.5° either side of the Greenwich meridian. The zones then move round the world east and west of Greenwich in 15° units, although some countries tweak them to fit local geography. They meet at the International Date Line. This more or less follows the 180° meridian and the eastern hemisphere is always one day ahead of the date in the western hemisphere.

Local time in a ship's log has its 'zone description', which is the number of hours that must be added or subtracted to find GMT. Time zones to the east of Greenwich cover the hours −1 to −12 and those to the west +1 to +12. In the 1950s zone Zero was given the letter Z, zones to the east were labelled A through M (missing out J), and zones to the west labelled M through Y. However, the usual convention is to describe zone time as Z (or Zulu) plus or minus the number of hours that must be added or subtracted to find GMT.

Time and the Navigator

Navigation depends on knowing the time, both local and GMT, and in timing intervals like the time taken to run a certain distance. There are alternatives to a watch. The first is the sun.

Time from the Sun

The Equation of Time

Solar time is based upon the apparent solar day, which is the time between two successive local noons at the same longitude. The length of the solar day varies, partly because the earth's orbit is an ellipse, and also because the earth's axis is tilted to the celestial equator.

The mean solar day is fixed at 24 hours, but the actual solar day can be nearly 22 seconds shorter or almost 29 seconds longer. These differences can build up to around 17 minutes early or 14 minutes late, (see Figure 10.1). The difference between apparent and mean solar time is called the equation of time:

Mean Solar Time = Apparent Solar Time +/− The Equation of Time

If you want greater accuracy and if you have a pocket calculator, the Equation of Time for any day can be found (approximately) using the equation:

Equation of Time = 9.87 * sin (2B) − 7.53 * cos (B) − 1.5 * sin (B)

Where:

$$B = 360 \times (N - 81)/364$$

$N =$ day number, January 1 $=$ Day 1 and count from there.

During daylight the best means of estimating the passage of time, as opposed to telling the time, is the sun's position. The sun rises in the east and travels westwards in a great arc reaching its zenith (highest point) at noon before setting in the west. There are 360° in a circle and in each hour the sun appears to travel 15°, which lets you divide the horizon into 15° (or hourly) blocks.

Equation of Time on	5th	15th	25th	Average Change (secs)
January	−5m 03s	−9m 10s	−12m 12s	20
February	−14m 01s	−14m 16s	−13m 18s	5
March	−11m 45s	−9m 13s	−6m 16s	16
April	−2m 57s	+0m 14s	+1m 56s	18
May	+3m 18s	+3m 44s	+3m 16s	4
June	+1m 46s	−0m 10s	−2m 20s	16
July	−4m 19s	−5m 46s	−6m 24s	20
August	5m 59s	−4m 33s	−2m 14s	11
September	+1m 05s	+4m 32s	+8m 04s	20
October	+11m 20s	14m 01s	+15m 47s	13
November	+16m 22s	15m 28s	+13m 11s	10
December	+9m 38s	+5m 09s	+0m 13s	27

(meaning of Av?)

10.1 Equation of Time

Local Noon

Local noon should give you one accurate time check each day but as the sun appears to hang around its zenith, timing local noon by observing the sun's zenith provides a hazy answer.

If you have a compass, know its deviation and your local variation, then in theory you can find local noon by determining when the sun points due south in the northern hemisphere, or due north in the southern hemisphere. In practice this works not very well, or not at all.

Local Noon by Equal Altitudes

If you must know the exact time of local noon and have a watch, then a little before noon, measure the altitude of the sun. Note the time from your watch. Wait until the sun is at exactly the same altitude after local noon and note the time (see Figure 10.2). Local noon is halfway between the two times.

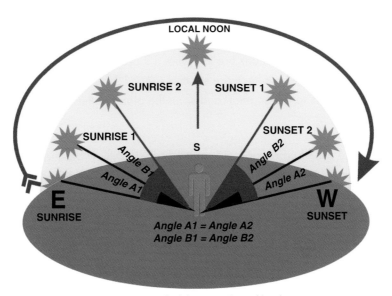

If you have a watch then you can find the exact time of local noon. Note the time when the sun rises and again when it sets. Local noon is exactly halfway between the two times. If you have made some easting or westing you will have to make allowance for distance sailed east or west.

It does not matter if your watch is wrong. It is the time difference that is important. You can still find local noon on the first day and put your watch right at noon on day two.

Alternatively, in the morning note the time and altitude of Sunrise 1 and Sunrise 2. Then in the evening when the sun is setting Sunset 1 is the time when the sun's altitude is equal to Sunrise 2. Local noon is halfway between these two times. It is the same for Sunrise 1 and Sunset 2. If your sums give different times for local noon from different sunrises and sunsets then take an average.

10.2 Finding Local Noon

Sunrise and Sunset

The time of sunrise is the time of local noon minus half the length of the daylight period, ie half the time between sunrise and sunset. The time of sunset is the time of local noon plus half the daylight period.

Making a Sundial

A sundial is not sufficiently precise for navigation but it may be useful for watch keeping and similar time checks. There are many kinds of sundial. The simplest to make is an equatorial sundial (instructions are in Figure 10.3). The gnomon is set at an angle equal to your latitude. The hour lines are spaced every 15° round the face of the dial, which is at right angles to the gnomon and so in the plane of the equator.

You will need:

- A piece of stiff card about 25 cm long and slightly wider than your protractor; you can also use wood, plastic, or metal providing you can mark the hours and drill a hole for the gnomon.

- A thin rod to act as a gnomon: this can be of wood, wire, knitting needle or even a drinking straw.

- A protractor to mark out the hours.

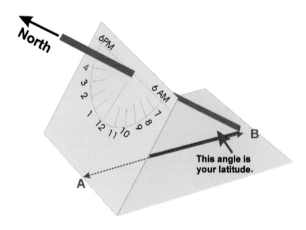

10.3 Making an Equatorial Sundial

To Make an Equatorial Sundial

1. One centimetre down from the top of your card, use the protractor to mark out the hours on both sides of the card. These are 15° apart.

2. Bend the card, or whatever, 15 centimetres down from the top of your hour dial.

3. At the centre of the hour dial, the point from where you measured the hour angles, make a hole just large enough to take the gnomon.

4. Insert the gnomon, making sure it is at 90° to the hour dial.

5. Slide the gnomon through until the angle it makes with the base is the same as your latitude. The easiest way to do this is to make AB the correct length for the angle. The length of AB is found by the formula:

AB = Cotangent of your latitude multiplied by 10.

In the northern hemisphere the gnomon points to true north and in the southern hemisphere to true south.

Time from the Stars

Two successive passages of a star over your position is one sidereal day. The sidereal day is 23 hours, 56 minutes 4.1 seconds of a mean solar day, which is usually rounded to 23 hours, 56 minutes and explains why the stars appear to rise about four minutes earlier each night (see Figure 10.4).

As night falls, find a star or constellation rising on the eastern horizon. It is not necessary to identify it. Like the sun it will travel across the sky to set in the west, and just as you can tell the time of day from the position of the sun in the sky, you can use a star to tell you time of night.

To estimate the actual time, use the stars in the Big Dipper and Cassiopeia. A line joining the stars called Ruchbah (Delta Cassiopeia) and Mizar (Zeta Ursa Major),

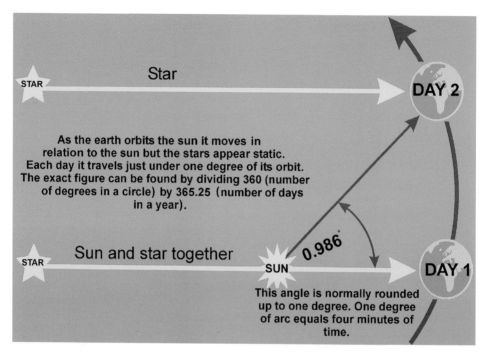

10.4 The Sidereal Day

shown in Figure 10.5, almost passes through the Pole Star and forms the hand of a 24-hour star clock. The tip of the hand is Ruchbah and when it is at the twelve o'clock position it is 0120 hours. Twelve hours later it points towards the six o'clock position and it is 1320 hours. Unlike its earthbound mechanical relatives the hand of this clock runs backwards.

Making a Nocturnal

A nocturnal is a star clock. They first appeared in the 13th century, and remained in use into the 19th century. Nocturnals came in three parts: a pointer, and separate date and hour discs rotating round a common centre. Using one involved sighting Polaris through a hole in the rivet or bolt holding the components together. A competent navigator would expect to find the time to within 15 minutes.

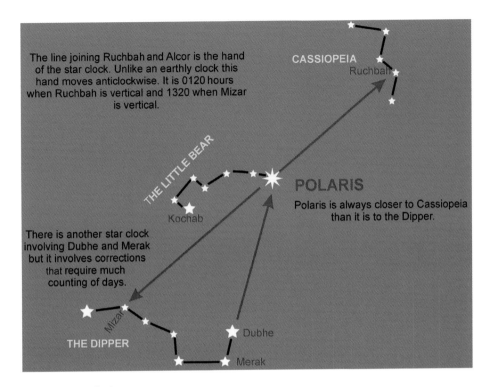

The line joining Ruchbah and Alcor is the hand of the star clock. Unlike an earthly clock this hand moves anticlockwise. It is 0120 hours when Ruchbah is vertical and 1320 when Mizar is vertical.

CASSIOPEIA

Ruchbah

THE LITTLE BEAR

Kochab

POLARIS

Polaris is always closer to Cassiopeia than it is to the Dipper.

There is another star clock involving Dubhe and Merak but it involves corrections that require much counting of days.

Mizar

THE DIPPER

Dubhe

Merak

10.5 The Star Clock

A simple nocturnal can be made from two discs. One is a clock face with the months round its edge and the other is a very simple star chart which fits inside the 24 hour clock face with midnight at the top and noon at the bottom (see chart and template shown in Figure 10.6 and Figure 10.7).

To use the nocturnal turn the clock face until the month is vertical. Next, hold the nocturnal up to the sky and turn the star chart until the stars on it match up with those in the sky. Finally, read the time.

Time from the Moon

The phase of the moon gives a clue to the time of day. A full moon is seen when the moon is on the opposite side of the earth from the sun, so the moon rises just as the sun

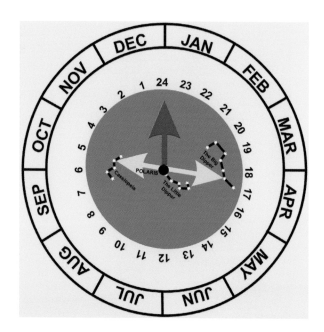

10.6 A Nocturnal

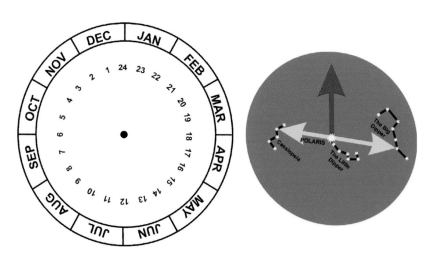

10.7 Templates for a Nocturnal

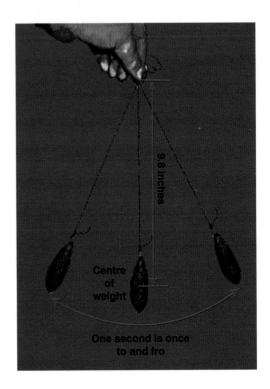

9.8 inches

Centre
of
weight

One second is once
to and fro

10.8 One Second Pendulum

sets, and sets as the sun rises. The next day, the moon will rise approximately 50 minutes later (because the moon has moved farther along on its orbit). A waning half moon rises at midnight, and a new moon at dawn. The moon moves about one of its diameters an hour. Knowing this and the time when it rose, it is possible to work out the time of night.

Counting Seconds

If you are unhappy counting the seconds to time casting the log then use a pendulum (see Figure 10.8). This is a weight (any weight) on the end of a line. Start it swinging and let it settle into its natural rhythm. When it has found its rhythm, the time it takes to swing back and forward once is called its period. How long this takes depends on the length of the string. A one-second pendulum has a string 24.9 cm (9.8 inches) long.

Dead reckoning and estimated positions

A Dead Reckoning Position

The Log Ship

Estimated Positions

The Traverse Board

In the 15th century the pioneers of the great European age of exploration made long ocean voyages using nothing but dead reckoning. Columbus relied on it for his 1492 voyage and reconstructions from his logs (he kept two) showed he managed an accuracy of well over 90%. If they practised the new art of celestial navigation they usually did this ashore, with the aim of obtaining positions to support claims of sovereignty and to update their charts.

A Dead Reckoning Position

A dead reckoning (DR) position is calculated by using the course steered and speed through the water as shown in Figure 11.1. We usually either over or underestimate our boat speed. Over a few hours an error of a fraction of a knot puts your position out by miles. If you steer a good course and get the tides and leeway right then you will be on track but ahead or behind your estimated position (EP). You still pick up your landfall, albeit either earlier or later than expected. It helps to have a log.

Dutchman's Log

Timing how long a piece of wood or scrap of paper takes to travel from bow to stern to find speed through the water works well in gentle weather but, as winds and seas increase, it becomes nonsensical.

If the chip travels 9 metres (30 feet) in five seconds then you are travelling at 2 metres (6 feet) per second (see Figure 11.2). Multiply this by 0.592. If you have no

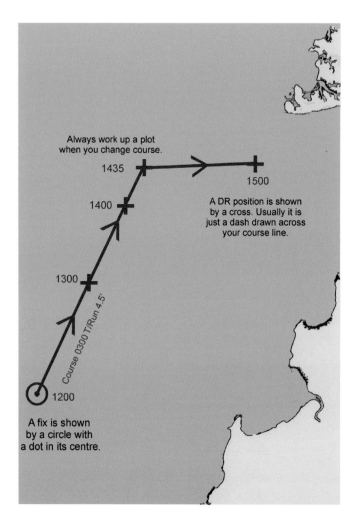

Always work up a plot
when you change course.

1435

1500

A DR position is shown
by a cross. Usually it is
just a dash drawn across
your course line.

1400

1300

Course 0300 T/Run 4.5'

1200

A fix is shown
by a circle with
a dot in its centre.

11.1 A DR Plot

calculator call it 0.6 and you have a speed of 3.6 knots. For those using a 10-metre distance, 2 metres per second becomes 3.9 knots when multiplied by 1.944.

You can skip the maths. If you are travelling at one knot you cover 0.5 metres (1.6878 feet) per second. Put marks along the toe rail at intervals of 1.7 feet and divide the number of marks the chip passes by the time it takes to pass them. You then

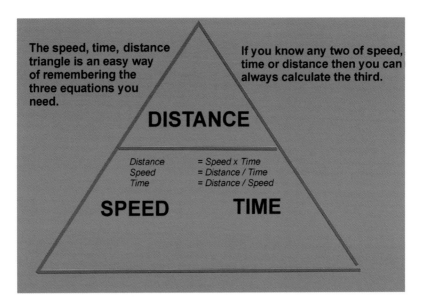

The speed, time, distance triangle is an easy way of remembering the three equations you need.

If you know any two of speed, time or distance then you can always calculate the third.

DISTANCE

Distance = Speed x Time
Speed = Distance / Time
Time = Distance / Speed

SPEED   **TIME**

11.2 Speed, Time, Distance Triangle

have your speed in knots. If your log passes nine marks in 2 seconds then you are making 4.5 knots.

If you choose a Dutchman's log it is best to:

1. Mark bow and stern to give a known accurately measured distance.

2. Have someone standing in the bows to throw the chip into the water ahead of the mark and shout, 'Now' when the chip passes the mark at the bow.

3. Have another crew member by the stern mark who starts timing on the cry of 'Now' and stops when the chip passes the stern mark.

The Log Ship

The log ship (see Figure 11.3) is nothing more than a board weighted so that when thrown overboard it stands upright and sits still in the water as it drags line off a reel.

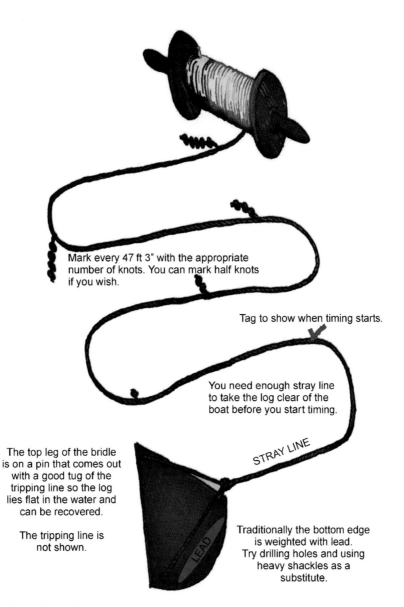

Mark every 47 ft 3" with the appropriate number of knots. You can mark half knots if you wish.

Tag to show when timing starts.

You need enough stray line to take the log clear of the boat before you start timing.

STRAY LINE

The top leg of the bridle is on a pin that comes out with a good tug of the tripping line so the log lies flat in the water and can be recovered.

The tripping line is not shown.

LEAD

Traditionally the bottom edge is weighted with lead. Try drilling holes and using heavy shackles as a substitute.

11.3 Traditional Log Ship

Once the spare line took the log clear of the ship, knots were tied in it every 14.5 metres (47 feet 3 inches). The number of knots that run out in 28 seconds is the speed through the water.

The rotator log was introduced in the 19th century but the log ship was still used on some US Navy ships as late as 1917. It is probably the best DIY log you could make.

Home-made Logs

The traditional log ship takes some carpentry but there are simpler alternatives. A bucket is great but is the devil to haul in. Small plastic beakers, filler funnels, mugs, and even empty cans work just as well, providing you use a light line and they are easy to recover. Even a bottle partly filled with seawater works.

Drill a hole near the lip of the can or beaker and drill another very small hole in the base to prevent trapped air bringing it to the surface and allowing it to skip along. A weight on the log line a few inches from the lip pulls it underwater, and another a few feet further back helps keep it down.

Allow 6 metres or so (20 feet) of slack before tying the first knot. If you tie one knot every 14.5 metres (47 feet 3 inches) you need around 122 metres (400 feet) of line to measure eight knots. If you do not have enough line then reduce the interval between knots to reduce the time. The spacing of knots is determined by

$$Space\ between\ knots = 1.6878 \times the\ timing\ interval$$

If you cut the time from 28 to six seconds then the knots are spaced at 3 metres (10.13 feet). After allowing for the spare line this takes about 31 metres (100 feet) of line.

The Timed Log Line

It is much simpler to time how long a fixed length of line takes to run out. Sixty feet (18 metres) plus 20 or so feet (6 metres) of slack will do. At the end of the spare line, tie a knot or make an easily seen mark to indicate the start of the timed run. After 60 feet tie another knot to mark the end of the run. Another few feet provides enough line to tie it

Line is
stowed
on an old
hand fishing
reel.

Any light line
will work.

Spare clevis pins
to ensure
plastic tumbler
stays underwater.

I used a plastic
glass; an empty can,
filler funnel or partly
filled bottle also work.
A tennis ball or quoit
does not.

11.4 A Home Made Timed Log
Line

to the pushpit (see Figure 11.4). This process gives consistent results to around 0.1 knot every time.

Casting the log every 30 minutes in a steady wind is a good rule of thumb, but if you are tacking, check your speed every tack.

Estimated Positions

An estimated position (EP) is your best position short of a fix. To turn a DR into an EP it is necessary to make allowances for tidal stream, currents, leeway, and the pricking of your thumbs, as shown in Figure 11.5.

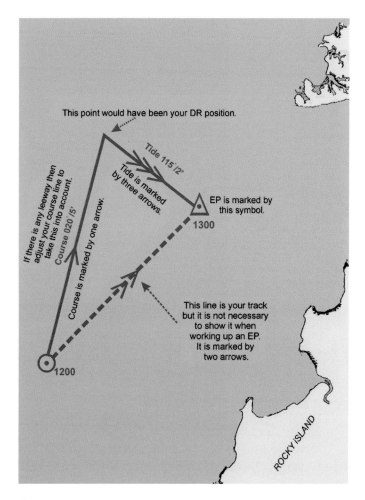

This point would have been your DR position.

Tide 115'/2'

Tide is marked by three arrows.

EP is marked by this symbol.

1300

If there is any leeway then adjust your course line to take this into account.

Course 020'/5'

Course is marked by one arrow.

This line is your track but it is not necessary to show it when working up an EP. It is marked by two arrows.

1200

ROCKY ISLAND

11.5 Estimated Position

Working out the expected rate and direction of the tidal stream should be part of your normal passage planning and it is a good idea to note this down rather than store it electronically. The actual tidal stream may be slightly different from that predicted, but an estimate based on good data is better than a wild guess.

If you are making an ocean passage, work out the rate and direction of any currents you are experiencing. These can differ from the figures in the pilot chart. We tend to assume the North Atlantic Drift is a smooth conveyor belt carrying you across the Atlantic from west to east. Not only can its rate vary but it is full of eddies and whirls that turn it back on itself.

Finding the actual current is easy when the GPS is working. Once a day, use the GPS to compare the course and distance made good over the last 24 hours with the course steered and distance sailed through the water. The difference is a mixture of leeway and current. Done as part of your noon position each day, it builds up a picture of the direction and rate of the current.

Otherwise it is back to rule of thumb. Currents are children of the wind. It is usual to assume that the rate of the current is 2% of the average wind speed over the last 24 hours. The Coriolis effect means that currents are deflected to the right, occasionally by as much as 30°, in the northern hemisphere and to the left in the southern hemisphere.

Leeway

If you are sailing with the wind on or forward of the beam, your boat makes leeway. Leeway is found by standing on the centre line of the boat, looking aft, and estimating the angle between the wake and the reciprocal of the course steered. It varies with boat speed, wind strength, and point sail. If you are uncertain, drop a line over the stern and watch it for a few minutes. The angle between the line and your wake is the leeway angle, illustrated in Figure 11.6.

The Traverse Board

It is important to keep a record of course and speed at intervals during each watch. For centuries seamen used a traverse board (see Chapter 5, Figure 5.8).

The upper half of a traverse board is a compass rose marked out in 32 points. Eight holes radiate out from the centre and are drilled along each point. In the centre are eight pegs, each on a length of string. Starting from the centre, each hole represents half an hour's sailing and the eight holes on each point made up one four-hour watch. Each half hour the Officer of the Watch (OOW) would place a peg in the hole corresponding to the course steered.

Wake

Compass course steered

Actual course

Diagrams illustrating leeway make it look simple. In practice, especially if there is a sea running, it can be quite difficult to decide on how much leeway you are making. We always like to think it is less than it really is.

In this example, with a big, breaking swell running, I used the log line to tell me how much leeway I was making.

11.6 Finding Leeway

The four lines of holes along the bottom of the board record speed. These are divided into two blocks. The number of horizontal holes in each block should be at least one greater that the boat's maximum speed. At the end of the first half hour the log would be cast and, counting from left to right, a peg inserted on the top line in the hole corresponding to that speed. This would be repeated each half hour. Each block represented two hours and together they made up a four-hour watch. At the end of each watch the traverse board gave the navigator the information needed to work up a DR.

Coastal navigation

As well as introducing its fair share of hazards to avoid, coastal sailing also provides lots of opportunities to work up a fix – or at least stay well clear of danger.

Distance to the Horizon

If you know the distance to your horizon then the instant anything comes over the horizon you know its distance off.

There are a lot of equations for calculating distance to the horizon. They all give much the same answer and most are based on Pythagoras and his right-angled triangle. You need only two: one working with the height in feet and one with the height in metres. Both give answers in nautical miles.

$$\text{Distance to Horizon} = 1.144 \times \sqrt{\text{Height of Eye in feet.}}$$

$$\text{Distance to Horizon} = 2.072 \sqrt{\text{Height of Eye in metres.}}$$

Dipping Distance

A dipping distance is when you just catch sight of the very top of a feature. If you know the height of the feature then you can calculate the distance from it to its horizon, add on the distance to your horizon, and you have the dipping distance (see Figure 12.1).

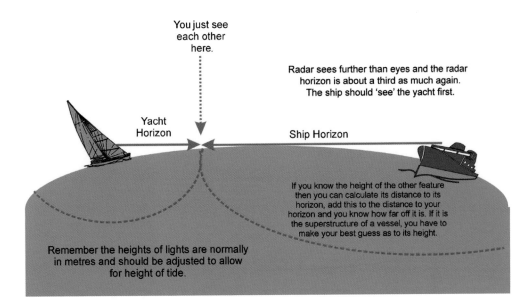

You just see
each other
here.

Radar sees further than eyes and the radar
horizon is about a third as much again.
The ship should 'see' the yacht first.

Yacht
Horizon

Ship Horizon

If you know the height of the other feature
then you can calculate its distance to its
horizon, add this to the distance to your
horizon and you know how far off it is. If it is
the superstructure of a vessel, you have to
make your best guess as to its height.

Remember the heights of lights are normally
in metres and should be adjusted to allow
for height of tide.

12.1 Dipping Distances

Dipping distances are a good example of when you may be working with the height of
your eye in feet, and the height of the feature in metres.

Geographic and Nominal Range of Lights

Using the range of a light as a means of judging distance off depends on which of its
four ranges you are using (see Figure 12.2). A light's geographical range is the
distance it can be seen in conditions of perfect visibility and usually equates to its
dipping distance.

Its visual range is the distance it can be made out against its background. This
varies with atmospheric conditions and sometimes is increased by using binoculars.

A light's luminous range is the distance it can be seen depending on the current
atmospheric conditions.

Its nominal range is the distance at which it can be seen when meteorlogical
visibility is 10 nautical miles. This is the range that appears on charts and in lists
of lights.

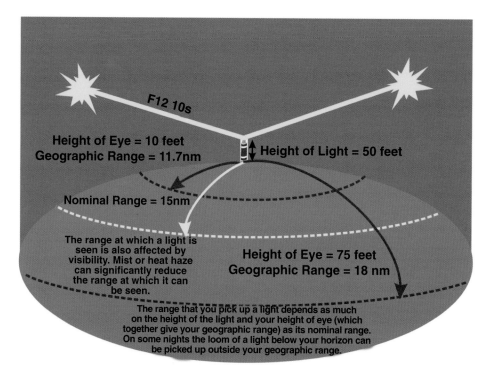

Height of Eye = 10 feet
Geographic Range = 11.7nm

F12 10s

Height of Light = 50 feet

Nominal Range = 15nm

The range at which a light is
seen is also affected by
visibility. Mist or heat haze
can significantly reduce
the range at which it can
be seen.

Height of Eye = 75 feet
Geographic Range = 18 nm

The range that you pick up a light depends as much
on the height of the light and your height of eye (which
together give your geographic range) as its nominal range.
On some nights the loom of a light below your horizon can
be picked up outside your geographic range.

12.2 Nominal and Geographic Range of Lights

Distance Off by Similar Triangles

When two triangles have internal angles of the same value they are called similar. One
characteristic of similar triangles is that although their sides have different lengths, they
are proportionate to each other. The ratio of any two sides in the first triangle equals
the ratio of the same sides in the second triangle. If you know the length of any three of
these four sides, finding the value of the fourth is straightforward.

You would like to know the distance between you and the lighthouse of a known
height. Hold a ruler at arm's length (57 centimetres) and measure the height of the
lighthouse on the ruler in centimetres. You now know three of your four sides and can
calculate the distance off (illustrated in Figure 12.3).

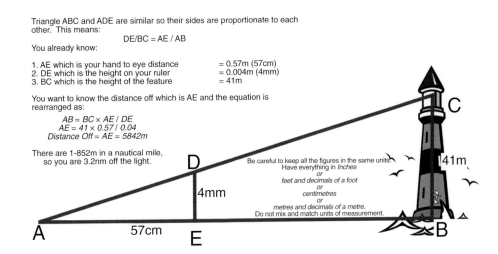

Triangle ABC and ADE are similar so their sides are proportionate to each other. This means:

DE/BC = AE / AB

You already know:

1. AE which is your hand to eye distance   = 0.57m (57cm)
2. DE which is the height on your ruler   = 0.004m (4mm)
3. BC which is the height of the feature   = 41m

You want to know the distance off which is AE and the equation is rearranged as:

AB = BC × AE / DE
AE = 41 × 0.57 / 0.04
Distance Off = AE = 5842m

There are 1-852m in a nautical mile, so you are 3.2nm off the light.

Be careful to keep all the figures in the same units.
Have everything in *Inches*
or
feet and decimals of a foot
or
centimetres
or
metres and decimals of a metre.
Do not mix and match units of measurement.

12.3 Distance Off by Similar Triangles

Clearing Distance by Similar Triangles

You can use similar triangles for a clearing distance. Suppose you wish to stay one mile off a light 41 metres high.

AC, which is your hand to eye distance $= 0.57$ metre.
AE, which is the distance off $= 1$ nautical mile $= 1852$ metres.
DE, which is the height of the feature $= 41$ metres.

You want to know BC, which is the height on your ruler.
By re-arranging the equation:

$$AC/BC = AE/DE$$

you get:

$$BC = DE \times AC/AE$$
$$BC = 41 \times .57/1852$$

Clearing Distance $= BC = 0.013 = 0.013m = 1.3$ *centimetres.*

Now you know that if the reading is less than 1.3 centimetres, then you are too close.

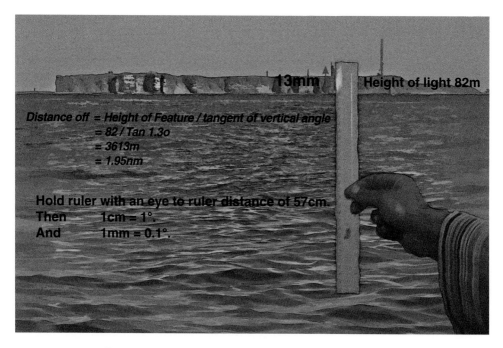

13mm

Height of light 82m

Distance off = Height of Feature / tangent of vertical angle
= 82 / Tan 1.3o
= 3613m
= 1.95nm

Hold ruler with an eye to ruler distance of 57cm.
Then   1cm = 1°.
And   1mm = 0.1°.

12.4 Distance Off by Vertical Angle

Distance Off by Vertical Angle

Alternatively you can find the distance off by vertical angle between the feature and the shore. Without a sextant to measure the angle hold a ruler 57cm from your eye (Figure 12.4) and your measurement in centimetres and millimetres is in degrees and decimals of a degree. The distance off is found using the equation:

Distance off = Height of feature/tangent of vertical angle.

Distance Off by Horizontal Angle

Measuring horizontal angles using a ruler (see Chapter 13) is easier than using a sextant and probably just as accurate.

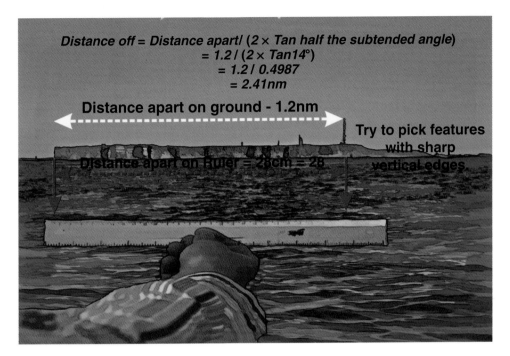

Distance off = Distance apart/ (2 × Tan half the subtended angle)
= 1.2 / (2 × Tan14°)
= 1.2 / 0.4987
= 2.41nm

Distance apart on ground - 1.2nm

Try to pick features with sharp vertical edges.

Distance apart on Ruler = 28cm = 28

12.5 Distance Off by Horizontal Angle

If you have two features that are a known distance apart, it is simple to calculate your distance off (Figure 12.5). The features could be the markers for a measured mile – two correctly identified charted features whose distance you know or can measure from the chart.

Distance Off by Winking

You can make a fair estimate of your distance off using the Wink Method (see Figure 12.6). This needs no instruments and little arithmetic and there is no maths using the appearance of features in judging distance off which can be surprisingly accurate (check what to look for in Figure 12.7).

Known distance 300 m

**Hold your arm out.
Place the edge of your finger
at one end of your known
distance.
Close one eye.**

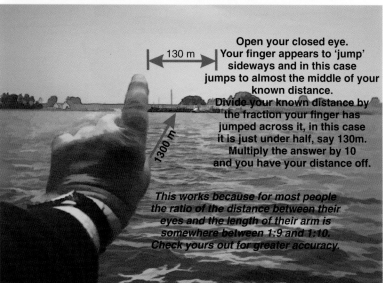

130 m

1300 m

**Open your closed eye.
Your finger appears to 'jump'
sideways and in this case
jumps to almost the middle of your
known distance.
Divide your known distance by
the fraction your finger has
jumped across it, in this case
it is just under half, say 130m.
Multiply the answer by 10
and you have your distance off.**

*This works because for most people
the ratio of the distance between their
eyes and the length of their arm is
somewhere between 1:9 and 1:10.
Check yours out for greater accuracy.*

12.6 The Wink Method or Distance Off

SERIAL	DETAIL	DISTANCE
1	Clothing can be seen and people's faces begin to be made out.	One cable (0.1 nm)
2	The colours on people's clothing can be made out.	0.25 nm
3	A person looks like a wooden post.	0.5 nm
4	Largish trees can be made out individually.	1.0 nm
5	Windows and chimneys can be made out on buildings.	2.0 nm
6	Large houses can be made out.	5.0 nm
7	Church towers and steeples become visible.	8.0 nm

12.7 Judging Distance

Distance Off by Horizon Angle

It is possible that you want to know your distance off a light, a headland or a buoy but do not know its height and so cannot use a vertical sextant angle. There is one other method that may work. Measure the angle between its waterline and the horizon. This is called distance off by horizon angle (see Figure 12.8).

Three points to note: firstly, if your height of eye is in feet then your answer is in feet; secondly, this is one of the rare occasions when the correction for dip is added to your reading; thirdly, working in small angles pushes home-made sextants to, and probably beyond, the limits of their accuracy. Do not expect too much.

Distance Off by Bearings

Take a bearing on a feature before it comes abeam, steer a steady course and note the distance run when it comes abeam. You can now calculate your distance off, as shown in Figure 12.9.

Doubling the Angle on the Bow

If, for some reason, it is not possible to bring the feature abeam then you can still get a fix by doubling the angle on the bow (see Figure 12.10).

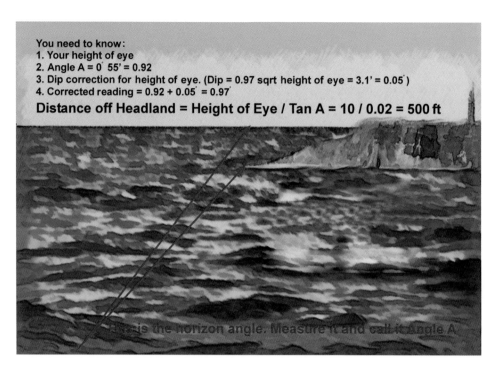

You need to know:
1. Your height of eye
2. Angle A = 0 55' = 0.92
3. Dip correction for height of eye. (Dip = 0.97 sqrt height of eye = 3.1' = 0.05')
4. Corrected reading = 0.92 + 0.05' = 0.97'

Distance off Headland = Height of Eye / Tan A = 10 / 0.02 = 500 ft

This is the horizon angle. Measure it and call it Angle A

12.8 Distance Off by Horizon Angle

A Bow and Beam Bearing

If you have no means of measuring bearings, you can still find your distance off by taking a Bow and Beam bearing. This is a special case of doubling the angle on the bow using angles you can judge by eye.

Note the log reading when the first relative bearing is 45°. When the feature comes abeam, ie, the relative angle is 90°, work out the distance sailed and you have the distance off (see Figure 12.11).

Relative Bearings

The bearings used are relative bearings. If you are steering 030° and take a bearing on a suitable feature of 080° then the bearing you double is the relative bearing of 50° and not the compass bearing.

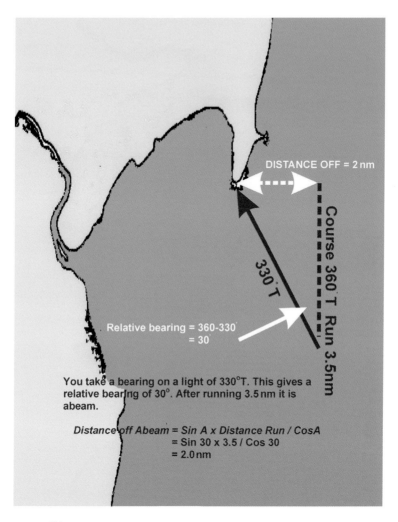

DISTANCE OFF = 2 nm

Course 360°T Run 3.5nm

330°T

Relative bearing = 360-330°
= 30°

You take a bearing on a light of 330°T. This gives a relative bearing of 30°. After running 3.5nm it is abeam.

Distance off Abeam = Sin A x Distance Run / CosA
= Sin 30 x 3.5 / Cos 30
= 2.0nm

12.9 Distance Off by Bearing

Distance Off by Echo Ranging

In fog, in inshore, cliffy waters you can try echo ranging for the distance off. This uses the time delay between the production of the sound and the arrival of its echo. This assumes that the speed of sound is a constant. It actually varies with the type of gas

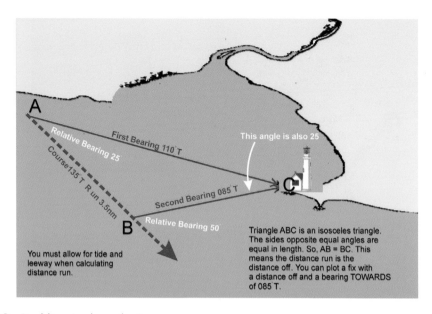

A

Relative Bearing 25°

First Bearing 110° T

This angle is also 25

Course 135° T R un 3.5nm

Second Bearing 085° T

B

Relative Bearing 50°

You must allow for tide and leeway when calculating distance run.

Triangle ABC is an isosceles triangle. The sides opposite equal angles are equal in length. So, AB = BC. This means the distance run is the distance off. You can plot a fix with a distance off and a bearing TOWARDS of 085° T.

12.10   Doubling Angle on the Bow

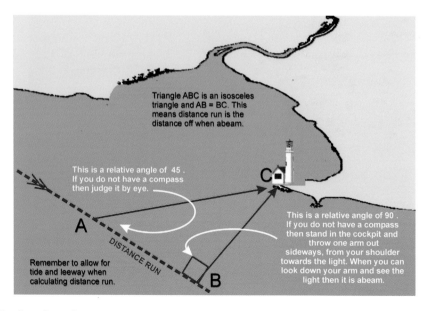

Triangle ABC is an isosceles triangle and AB = BC. This means distance run is the distance off when abeam.

This is a relative angle of 45°. If you do not have a compass then judge it by eye.

A

DISTANCE RUN

B

Remember to allow for tide and leeway when calculating distance run.

This is a relative angle of 90°. If you do not have a compass then stand in the cockpit and throw one arm out sideways, from your shoulder towards the light. When you can look down your arm and see the light then it is abeam.

12.11   Four Point Fix

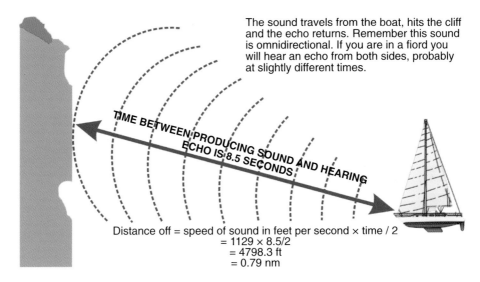

The sound travels from the boat, hits the cliff and the echo returns. Remember this sound is omnidirectional. If you are in a fiord you will hear an echo from both sides, probably at slightly different times.

TIME BETWEEN PRODUCING SOUND AND HEARING ECHO IS 8.5 SECONDS

Distance off = speed of sound in feet per second × time / 2
= 1129 × 8.5/2
= 4798.3 ft
= 0.79 nm

12.12 Echo Ranging

and its temperature, and at 21°C the answer is 669 knots (1129 feet per second or 344 metres per second). In water the speed of sound is 2877 knots (1480 metres per second).

You now know the speed at which your blast on the foghorn travels to the cliff, bounces off and returns, and the time this return journey took. Do your sums, halve the answer and you have your distance off (see Figure 12.12). A variation is finding out how far you are from an electrical storm. Time the interval between a flash of lightning and its thunder arriving. Do your sums, but this time do not divide the answer by two, and hope the storm is moving away from you.

Home-made sextants

You must be able to measure angles. Hands and fingers (see Figure 13.1) are one answer. Normally the angle subtended by a finger at an arm's length is taken as one degree but it varies from person to person. The Chinese called this measurement a *chih* and there were 224 chihs (1 chih = 1.6°) in a circle. Arabs called it an *issabah*. Nature places a limit on the size of angle you can measure au naturel. Unless you have abnormally large hands it is around 30–40°.

A word of warning: people go blind staring into the sun. Unless you use a shadow astrolabe or a sun shadow board, or have some very good shades, stick to stars, however tempting it is to take a sun sight.

The Astrolabe

Marine astrolabes were about four inches in diameter with a scale marked in degrees, and heavy to make them steady. They were horribly inaccurate, partly because accuracy is a function of size but also because it took three men to use it: one person held it, another took the sight, and a third read it. When Vasco da Gama, on his way towards the Cape of Good Hope, reached St Helena Bay, he went ashore with a large wooden astrolabe because he had been unable to take a sight on the voyage south. Some complicated gadgets aimed to make the astrolabe reliable at sea. They all failed but probably kept the crew amused. Less than 100 marine astrolabes are known to have survived, probably because most were thrown overboard in frustration.

A shadow astrolabe (see Figure 13.2 and Figure 13.2b) lets you take a noon altitude without staring into the sun. All you have to do is hang it up, watch the shadow

13.1

climb towards the horizontal and note the highest reading before it starts dropping back. Do not expect much.

The Sun Shadow Board

The Vikings used a sun shadow board to find latitude. It was nothing more than a small wooden disc with a number of concentric circles representing different latitudes and a gnomon whose height could be adjusted for the time of year.

At noon the sun shadow board would be placed in a tub of water with the gnomon set to the correct date. If the shadow it cast at noon was beyond the desired latitude they were too far north, and if it did not reach it, then they were too far south.

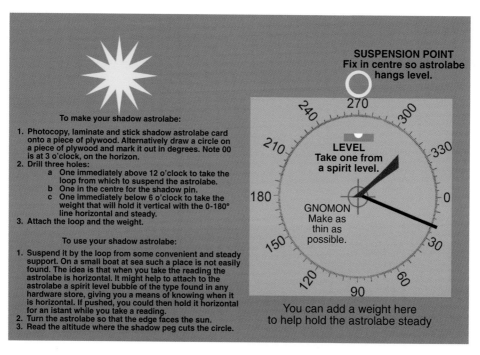

To make your shadow astrolabe:

1. Photocopy, laminate and stick shadow astrolabe card onto a piece of plywood. Alternatively draw a circle on a piece of plywood and mark it out in degrees. Note 00 is at 3 o'clock, on the horizon.
2. Drill three holes:
   - a One immediately above 12 o'clock to take the loop from which to suspend the astrolabe.
   - b One in the centre for the shadow pin.
   - c One immediately below 6 o'clock to take the weight that will hold it vertical with the 0-180° line horizontal and steady.
3. Attach the loop and the weight.

To use your shadow astrolabe:

1. Suspend it by the loop from some convenient and steady support. On a small boat at sea such a place is not easily found. The idea is that when you take the reading the astrolabe is horizontal. It might help to attach to the astrolabe a spirit level bubble of the type found in any hardware store, giving you a means of knowing when it is horizontal. If pushed, you could then hold it horizontal for an istant while you take a reading.
2. Turn the astrolabe so that the edge faces the sun.
3. Read the altitude where the shadow peg cuts the circle.

SUSPENSION POINT
Fix in centre so astrolabe hangs level.

LEVEL
Take one from a spirit level.

GNOMON
Make as thin as possible.

You can add a weight here to help hold the astrolabe steady

13.2 Making and Using a Shadow Astrolabe

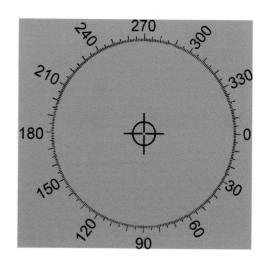

13.2b Template for Sun Shadow Board

A sun shadow board is difficult to make and there are other, easier, more accurate ways of checking latitude.

The Latitude Hook

The latitude hook was a favourite of the Polynesians. One piece of bamboo was twisted into a small loop. Another formed a crosspiece, sometimes called the pointer. The distance between the loop and the crosspiece varied with latitude. When held at arm's length with the crosspiece on the horizon and the Pole star in the centre of the loop you were on the latitude of your destination. There were different latitude hooks for different destinations. Making a latitude hook is easy. A piece of wire is a good alternative to bamboo, as shown in Figure 13.3.

One evening when you are on your chosen latitude and before you need to use Crash Bag Navigation, go on deck, hold the latitude hook at arm's length, put Polaris in the centre of the loop, align the crosspiece with the horizon and thereafter you will be able to check if you are on your chosen latitude. If you change your latitude, move the crosspiece or make a new latitude hook.

The Kamál

Arab navigators used the Kamál (meaning *Guide*) which works on the same principles as the latitude hook. It was a small wooden board with a hole through its centre. A knotted line was passed through the hole. The spacing of the knots corresponded to the known latitude of different ports. The navigator put the knot for his destination between his teeth, and held the Kamál out with the bottom edge on the horizon. When Polaris touched the top of the board he was on the latitude of his destination. The Chinese also used the Kamál but with a line of a fixed length and a selection of different sized boards to measure different angles. As a Kamál is held at a constant distance from the eye it is more accurate than the latitude hook.

The version of the Kamál described here (and shown in Figure 13.4) works in degrees and allows you to measure horizontal as well as vertical angles. It is nothing

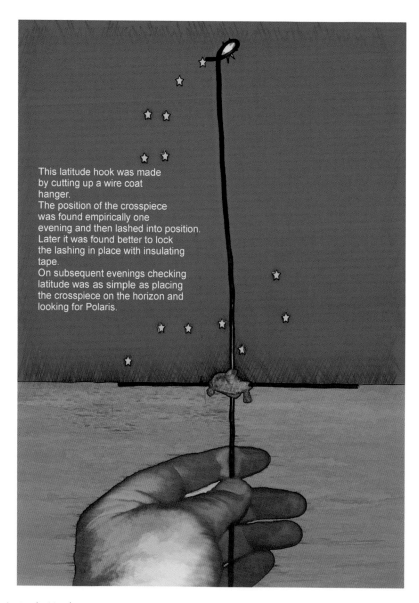

This latitude hook was made by cutting up a wire coat hanger.
The position of the crosspiece was found empirically one evening and then lashed into position. Later it was found better to lock the lashing in place with insulating tape.
On subsequent evenings checking latitude was as simple as placing the crosspiece on the horizon and looking for Polaris.

13.3 Latitude Hook

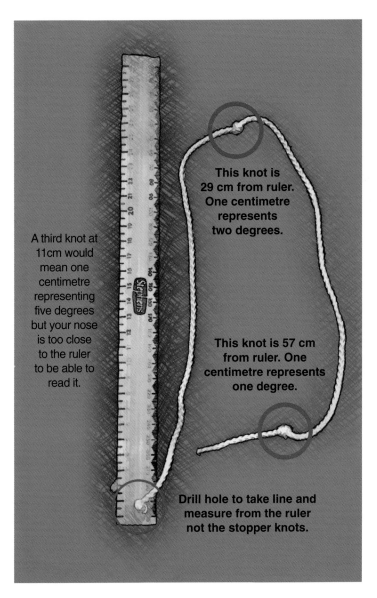

A third knot at 11cm would mean one centimetre representing five degrees but your nose is too close to the ruler to be able to read it.

This knot is 29 cm from ruler. One centimetre represents two degrees.

This knot is 57 cm from ruler. One centimetre represents one degree.

Drill hole to take line and measure from the ruler not the stopper knots.

13.4 Simple Kamál

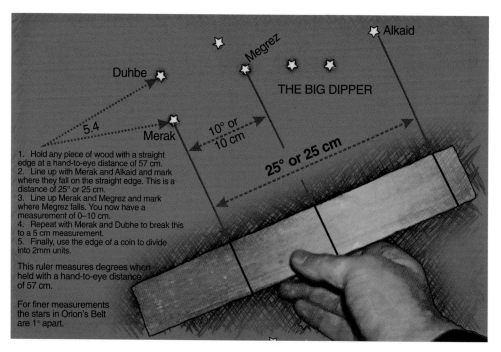

Alkaid

Megrez

Duhbe

THE BIG DIPPER

5.4

Merak

10° or
10 cm

25° or 25 cm

1. Hold any piece of wood with a straight edge at a hand-to-eye distance of 57 cm.
2. Line up with Merak and Alkaid and mark where they fall on the straight edge. This is a distance of 25° or 25 cm.
3. Line up Merak and Megrez and mark where Megrez falls. You now have a measurement of 0–10 cm.
4. Repeat with Merak and Dubhe to break this to a 5 cm measurement.
5. Finally, use the edge of a coin to divide into 2mm units.

This ruler measures degrees when held with a hand-to-eye distance of 57 cm.

For finer measurements the stars in Orion's Belt are 1° apart.

13.5 Making a Ruler

more than a shop-bought centimetre ruler with a hole drilled to take a line. A knot is tied in the line 57centimetres from the ruler.

To use it, the knot is placed between your teeth and the Kamál held straight out with the line horizontal, the Kamál vertical and zero on the horizon. The angle is then read off. One centimetre equals one degree and one millimetre 0.1°.

If you do not have a ruler it is still possible to make a Kamál out of a length of wood and calibrate it, using stars whose separation in degrees you know (see Figure 13.5). If you require very precise measurements, the moon (and the sun) are both about half a degree across.

The Quadrant

Do not confuse this with the forerunner of the sextant. It is a 90° protractor with a plumb line hanging from its vertex. Polaris is sighted along one edge and the angle where the line cuts the scale is read. As sailors were more interested in the latitude of a place rather than latitude as a number, some early quadrants replaced the degree markings with the names of ports.

The advantage of the quadrant is that you do not need to see the horizon. Most marine quadrants used a radius of 10–12 inches (30 centimetres) but the larger the quadrant the greater the spacing between degree markings and the greater its accuracy (see Figure 13.6). Tycho Brahe, the 16th century Danish astronomer, had one that filled a room.

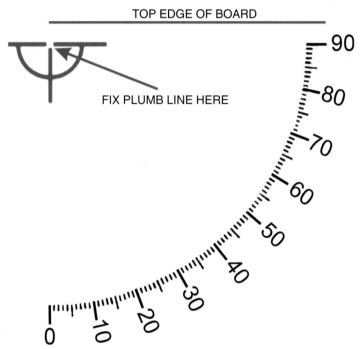

1. Photocopy scale, laminate and stick on piece of plywood that has at least one edge absolutely straight. This edge is the top edge of your quadrant.
2. Fix sights along top edge. These can be small nails, small brass eyes, or a narrow tube. The further apart the fore and rear sights the more accurate your sighting.
3. Attach plumb line. Use as heavy a weight as possible.
4. Some sort of handle to hold is preferable but not absolutely essential.

13.6 Quadrant

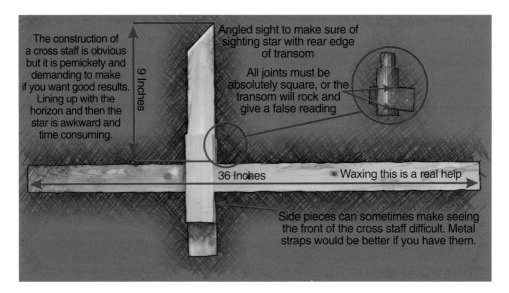

The construction of a cross staff is obvious but it is pernickety and demanding to make if you want good results. Lining up with the horizon and then the star is awkward and time consuming.

9 Inches

Angled sight to make sure of sighting star with rear edge of transom

All joints must be absolutely square, or the transom will rock and give a false reading

36 Inches

Waxing this is a real help

Side pieces can sometimes make seeing the front of the cross staff difficult. Metal straps would be better if you have them.

13.7 Traditional Type Cross Staff

The Cross Staff

It consists of a staff, usually about 36 inches (91.5 centimetres) long, and a shorter crosspiece called the transom, which slides up and down the staff to measure altitudes. The earliest known description comes from Persia in the 11th century. The first western description is by Levi ben Gerson in 1342 but it was 1485 before the German mathematician and navigator, Martin Behaim, took it to sea when he sailed down the east African coast with the Portuguese explorer, Diego Cao.

To make a cross staff you will need three lengths of wood: one for the staff and two for the transom as shown in Figure 13.7. A very crude cross staff can be made by lashing two pieces of wood (one long, one short) at right angles to each other.

Using a cross staff means the observer must observe the horizon and the celestial body simultaneously. This introduces ocular parallax, the scientific term for looking in two places at once. This effect can be reduced somewhat by using only one side of the transom, and placing the tip of the staff on the horizon instead of the bottom of the transom. You may find the 'long gun' cross staff easier to hold and use (see Figure 13.8) particularly at night.

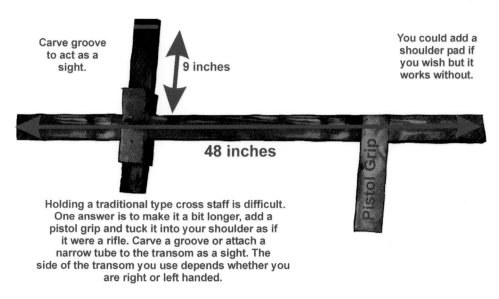

Carve groove
to act as a
sight.

9 inches

You could add a
shoulder pad if
you wish but it
works without.

48 inches

Pistol Grip

Holding a traditional type cross staff is difficult.
One answer is to make it a bit longer, add a
pistol grip and tuck it into your shoulder as if
it were a rifle. Carve a groove or attach a
narrow tube to the transom as a sight. The
side of the transom you use depends whether you
are right or left handed.

13.8 Long Gun Cross Staff

Polaris is sighted along the staff and the transom then slides up or down the staff until it fills the sky between the horizon and Polaris. The tangent of the angle between the top of the transom and the eye end of the staff gives the altitude of Polaris (see Figure 13.9). The fact that it resembles a crossbow caused navigators to talk about 'shooting the sun'.

Calibrating the Cross Staff

Cross staffs came with three or four transoms of varying lengths, each measuring a different range of angles. The scale for each transom would be engraved along its own side of the staff.

Calibrate your cross staff using the figures in Figure 13.10. If you have no means of measuring inches or centimetres, use five coins taped together as your base unit. Calibrating a cross staff makes it obvious that it is easiest to use for altitudes of between 30–60°.

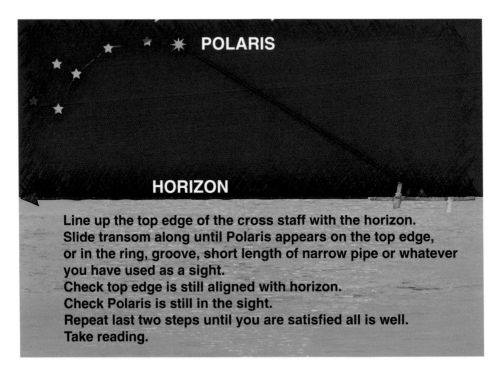

POLARIS

HORIZON

Line up the top edge of the cross staff with the horizon.
Slide transom along until Polaris appears on the top edge,
or in the ring, groove, short length of narrow pipe or whatever
you have used as a sight.
Check top edge is still aligned with horizon.
Check Polaris is still in the sight.
Repeat last two steps until you are satisfied all is well.
Take reading.

13.9 Using the Cross Staff

The Back Staff

To avoid staring into the sun navigators fitted a small box with a slot called a Dutch
Shoe to the transom, held the cross staff backwards and stood with their back to the
sun. The slot threw a sharp line of sunlight on the staff when the sun was 'on'.

A variety of backwards-shooting instruments soon appeared. The best known was
designed by John Davis, a 16th-century English navigator whose name is remembered
in the Davis Strait. He described his design in *The Seaman's Secrets*. It employs the
same principles as the cross staff but allows the observer to stand with his back to the
sun and uses the shadows it casts to measure altitude. This also eliminated ocular
parallax but, as stars cast no shadows, it could not be used at night, until the mirrored
back staff was introduced. Davies' back staff remained in use for over 200 years

	Distance from Eye in Inches						Distance from Eye in Centimetres		
Degrees	**6 inch Transom**	**7 inch Transom**	**8 inch Transom**	**9 inch Transom**	**tangent**	**Degrees**	**15 cm Transom**	**18cm Transom**	**20cm Transom**
10	34.0	39.7	45.4	51.0	0.1763	10	85.1	102.1	113.4
11	30.9	36.0	41.2	46.3	0.1944	11	77.2	92.6	102.9
12	28.2	32.9	37.6	42.3	0.2126	12	70.6	84.7	94.1
13	26.0	30.3	34.7	39.0	0.2309	13	65.0	78.0	86.6
14	24.1	28.1	32.1	36.1	0.2493	14	60.2	72.2	80.2
15	22.4	26.1	29.9	33.6	0.2679	15	56.0	67.2	74.6
16	20.9	24.4	27.9	31.4	0.2867	16	52.3	62.8	69.7
17	19.6	22.9	26.2	29.4	0.3057	17	49.1	58.9	65.4
18	18.5	21.5	24.6	27.7	0.3249	18	46.2	55.4	61.6
19	17.4	20.3	23.2	26.1	0.3443	19	43.6	52.3	58.1
20	16.5	19.2	22.0	24.7	0.3640	20	41.2	49.5	54.9
21	15.6	18.2	20.8	23.4	0.3839	21	39.1	46.9	52.1
22	14.9	17.3	19.8	22.3	0.4040	22	37.1	44.6	49.5
23	14.1	16.5	18.8	21.2	0.4245	23	35.3	42.4	47.1
24	13.5	15.7	18.0	20.2	0.4452	24	33.7	40.4	44.9
25	12.9	15.0	17.2	19.3	0.4663	25	32.2	38.6	42.9
26	12.3	14.4	16.4	18.5	0.4877	26	30.8	36.9	41.0
27	11.8	13.7	15.7	17.7	0.5095	27	29.4	35.3	39.3
28	11.3	13.2	15.0	16.9	0.5317	28	28.2	33.9	37.6
29	10.8	12.6	14.4	16.2	0.5543	29	27.1	32.5	36.1
30	10.4	12.1	13.9	15.6	0.5774	30	26.0	31.2	34.6
31	10.0	11.6	13.3	15.0	0.6009	31	25.0	30.0	33.3
32	9.6	11.2	12.8	14.4	0.6249	32	24.0	28.8	32.0
33	9.2	10.8	12.3	13.9	0.6494	33	23.1	27.7	30.8
34	8.9	10.4	11.9	13.3	0.6745	34	22.2	26.7	29.7
35	8.6	10.0	11.4	12.9	0.7002	35	21.4	25.7	28.6
36	8.3	9.6	11.0	12.4	0.7265	36	20.6	24.8	27.5
37	8.0	9.3	10.6	11.9	0.7536	37	19.9	23.9	26.5
38	7.7	9.0	10.2	11.5	0.7813	38	19.2	23.0	25.6
39	7.4	8.6	9.9	11.1	0.8098	39	18.5	22.2	24.7
40	7.2	8.3	9.5	10.7	0.8391	40	17.9	21.5	23.8
41	6.9	8.1	9.2	10.4	0.8693	41	17.3	20.7	23.0
42	6.7	7.8	8.9	10.0	0.9004	42	16.7	20.0	22.2
43	6.4	7.5	8.6	9.7	0.9325	43	16.1	19.3	21.4
44	6.2	7.2	8.3	9.3	0.9657	44	15.5	18.6	20.7
45	6.0	7.0	8.0	9.0	1.0000	45	15.0	18.0	20.0
46	5.8	6.8	7.7	8.7	1.0355	46	14.5	17.4	19.3
47	5.6	6.5	7.5	8.4	1.0724	47	14.0	16.8	18.7
48	5.4	6.3	7.2	8.1	1.1106	48	13.5	16.2	18.0
49	5.2	6.1	7.0	7.8	1.1504	49	13.0	15.6	17.4
50	5.0	5.9	6.7	7.6	1.1918	50	12.6	15.1	16.8
51	4.9	5.7	6.5	7.3	1.2349	51	12.1	14.6	16.2
52	4.7	5.5	6.3	7.0	1.2799	52	11.7	14.1	15.6
53	4.5	5.3	6.0	6.8	1.3270	53	11.3	13.6	15.1
54	4.4	5.1	5.8	6.5	1.3764	54	10.9	13.1	14.5
55	4.2	4.9	5.6	6.3	1.4281	55	10.5	12.6	14.0

13.10 Calibrating a Cross Staff (*continued overleaf*)

56	4.0	4.7	5.4	6.1	1.4826	56	10.1	12.1	13.5
57	3.9	4.5	5.2	5.8	1.5399	57	9.7	11.7	13.0
58	3.7	4.4	5.0	5.6	1.6003	58	9.4	11.2	12.5
59	3.6	4.2	4.8	5.4	1.6643	59	9.0	10.8	12.0
60	3.5	4.0	4.6	5.2	1.7321	60	8.7	10.4	11.5
61	3.3	3.9	4.4	5.0	1.8040	61	8.3	10.0	11.1
62	3.2	3.7	4.3	4.8	1.8807	62	8.0	9.6	10.6
63	3.1	3.6	4.1	4.6	1.9626	63	7.6	9.2	10.2
64	2.9	3.4	3.9	4.4	2.0503	64	7.3	8.8	9.8
65	2.8	3.3	3.7	4.2	2.1445	65	7.0	8.4	9.3
66	2.7	3.1	3.6	4.0	2.2460	66	6.7	8.0	8.9
67	2.5	3.0	3.4	3.8	2.3559	67	6.4	7.6	8.5
68	2.4	2.8	3.2	3.6	2.4751	68	6.1	7.3	8.1
69	2.3	2.7	3.1	3.5	2.6051	69	5.8	6.9	7.7
70	2.2	2.5	2.9	3.3	2.7475	70	5.5	6.6	7.3
71	2.1	2.4	2.8	3.1	2.9042	71	5.2	6.2	6.9
72	1.9	2.3	2.6	2.9	3.0777	72	4.9	5.8	6.5
73	1.8	2.1	2.4	2.8	3.2709	73	4.6	5.5	6.1
74	1.7	2.0	2.3	2.6	3.4874	74	4.3	5.2	5.7
75	1.6	1.9	2.1	2.4	3.7321	75	4.0	4.8	5.4
76	1.5	1.7	2.0	2.2	4.0108	76	3.7	4.5	5.0
77	1.4	1.6	1.8	2.1	4.3315	77	3.5	4.2	4.6
78	1.3	1.5	1.7	1.9	4.7046	78	3.2	3.8	4.3
79	1.2	1.4	1.6	1.7	5.1446	79	2.9	3.5	3.9
80	1.1	1.2	1.4	1.6	5.6713	80	2.6	3.2	3.5
81	1.0	1.1	1.3	1.4	6.3138	81	2.4	2.9	3.2
82	0.8	1.0	1.1	1.3	7.1154	82	2.1	2.5	2.8
83	0.7	0.9	1.0	1.1	8.1443	83	1.8	2.2	2.5
84	0.6	0.7	0.8	0.9	9.5144	84	1.6	1.9	2.1
85	0.5	0.6	0.7	0.8	11.4301	85	1.3	1.6	1.7

13.10 (*Continued*)

before it was eventually displaced by the octant and is the first navigational instrument whose inventor is known.

Some of these remarkably simple instruments can give acceptable results. The Kamál is the simplest. A shadow astrolabe allows you take noon sights without staring into the sun. A sun shadow board confirms your latitude, but you may obtain better results using a quadrant or a cross staff. However, the instrument that gives you the best results is the one you are most comfortable using.

Sextant corrections

DIP

Refraction

Horizon Sights

Parallax

Semi-Diameter

Angles measured with your home-made sextant, however inaccurate, ought to be corrected for dip, refraction, and if you use the sun, semi-diameter. Each correction is small but they add up, and applying these corrections gives a better position.

DIP

Dip depends on how high your eye is above sea level. It applies to sights taken with a Kamál or cross staff but not a quadrant or shadow astrolabe. The equation for dip in normal atmospheric conditions is:

> *Dip = 0.97 × the square root of the height of eye in feet*
> *If you do not have a calculator then you can round 0.97 up to 1.0.*

If you reckon that your eye is 10 feet above sea level then it is:

$$Dip = 0.97 \times Square\ Root\ of\ 10$$
$$= 0.97 \times 3.2$$
$$= 3.1'.$$

Dip is always (well, nearly always) negative and subtracted from your reading.

Refraction

Refraction is caused by light bending as it passes from the vacuum of space to the earth's atmosphere, making the sun and the stars look higher in the sky than they are. You see exactly the same phenomena when you poke a stick into water. How much the light bends varies with the amount of air that it passes through. The higher the sun or star, the less air there is. If it is low in the sky you are looking at it through more air. Refraction is always greater for sights taken when the celestial body is low in the sky. Refraction is always negative and subtracted from your observed angle.

The equation for mean refraction at standard temperature and pressure is daunting and given all the other sources of error surrounding readings with home-made sextants it is easier to use the following table:

Altitude	Correction
0°	−34′
5–6°	−9′
6–7°	−8′
7–8°	−7′
8–10°	−6′
10–12°	−5′
12–15°	−4′
15–21°	−3′
21–33°	−2′
33–63°	−1′
63–90°	0

Horizon Sights

The refraction for 0° is included in the above table in a situation where you have an accurate watch, tables and an almanac, but no sextant.

A horizon sight is when a celestial body just touches the horizon. If you use the sun you take the sight when either the upper or lower limb reaches the horizon. A horizon sight has an apparent altitude of 0° and is worked out just like any other. Be warned. Horizon sights are famous for their inaccuracy, mostly because of the problems of allowing for refraction below altitudes of 5°.

Parallax

Parallax is the difference between what you would see if you were standing at the middle of the earth – where angles should be measured – and between measuring the angle for real on the surface.

Parallax is included in the combined correction in the Nautical Almanac but there is no easy way for the Crash Bag Navigator to calculate it. For the sun and stars it is small enough to be ignored. By comparison the moon is so close to the earth its parallax can be significant. When overhead, its parallax is zero. When it is on the horizon its parallax is about a degree.

Semi-Diameter

The altitude of the sun should be measured from its centre, but it is difficult to decide exactly where its centre lies. Measure either from the bottom (lower limb) or top (upper limb) of the sun and apply a small correction. The sun's semi-diameter varies from a minimum of 15' 46" to a maximum of 16' 18" with a mean of 15' 59".6. So add 16' when you measure to the lower limb and subtract 16' if you measure to the upper limb. Semi-diameter applies only to sun sights but not sun sights taken by a shadow astrolabe.

Combining the Corrections

Starting with your measured angle, usually called *Hs*, which stands for Height Sextant, applying these corrections will give your observed or corrected altitude, usually called Height Observed or *Ho*.

$$Ho = Hs - dip - refraction +/- semi\text{-}diameter \text{ (if using the sun)}.$$

Meridian sights

A meridian sight has a lot going for it. First, as long as you can see it and know its declination you can use any celestial body. Secondly, although it helps to know the time, this is not absolutely essential. You can estimate when a body is at its zenith without a watch. Thirdly, you do not need complicated sight reduction tables or maths. Fourthly, it will always give you a position line, which is your latitude.

When you take the sun's altitude at noon you are measuring the angle between your horizon and the sun's zenith (see Figure 15.1). The angle between your horizon and your zenith is always 90°.

If you subtract the altitude of the sun, whatever it is, from 90° you get another angle, which is called the zenith distance. This is true of any celestial body and the zenith distance of any celestial body plus its altitude always comes to 90°. When a celestial body is at its zenith, the angle between a line from the centre of the earth to the body and the equator is its declination. Where this line passes through the surface of the earth it is on a parallel of latitude that has exactly the same value as the body's declination, as shown in Figure 15.2.

Your latitude, which is what you wish to discover, is your angular distance north or south of the equator (see Figure 15.3).

Put these three facts together and when you are in the northern hemisphere and a body has a northerly declination, then your latitude is your zenith distance plus declination and when the declination is southerly then your latitude is your zenith distance, minus declination (see Figure 15.4).

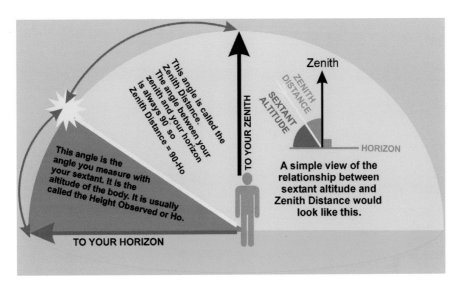

15.1 Zenith Distance

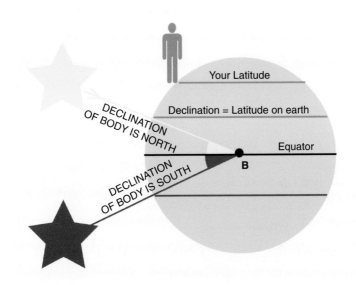

15.2

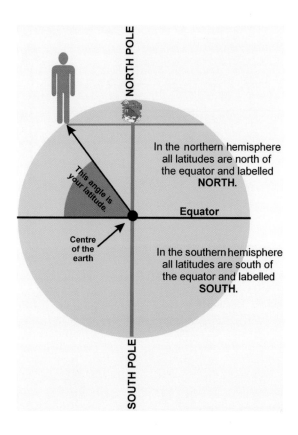

NORTH POLE

This angle is your latitude.

In the northern hemisphere all latitudes are north of the equator and labelled **NORTH.**

Equator

Centre of the earth

In the southern hemisphere all latitudes are south of the equator and labelled **SOUTH.**

SOUTH POLE

15.3

In the southern hemisphere it is all back to front so the general rule for both hemispheres is:

Latitude = Zenith Distance:

+ Declination when both it and your position have the same name ie both NORTH or both SOUTH.

− Declination when it and your position have different names.

A star's declination is fixed but the sun's changes daily because the tilt in the earth's axis makes it look as if the sun travels between the northern and southern hemispheres according to the season of the year. It reaches its furthest north (23.5°N) on the summer solstice. Then changing its declination daily it travels south to 23.5°S in

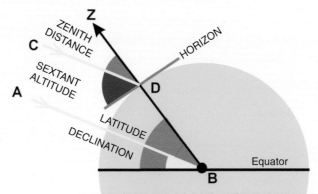

DECLINATION AND POSITION BOTH NORTH LATITUDE
Since AB and CD are parallel to each other
then
Angle ABZ = CDZ = Zenith Distance.
By Inspection
Latitude = Zenith Distance + Declination.

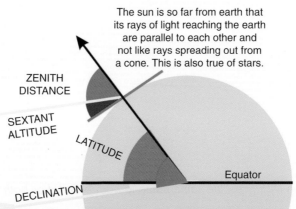

The sun is so far from earth that
its rays of light reaching the earth
are parallel to each other and
not like rays spreading out from
a cone. This is also true of stars.

DECLINATION SOUTH AND POSITION NORTH LATITUDE
Since AB and CD are parallel to each other
then
Angle ABZ = CDZ = Zenith Distance.
By Inspection
Latitude = Zenith Distance – Declination.

15.4 A Meridian Sight

time for the winter solstice. To calculate your noon latitude you must know the sun's declination on the day you take your sextant reading.

Your observed altitude must also be corrected for dip, refraction, and if you are using the sun, semi-diameter. The final equation for your noon sight is:

Latitude = 90 − observed altitude − dip − refraction + / − declination

+/ − semi-diameter.

Latitude from Polaris

Latitude from Polaris

Latitude from Circumpolar Stars

Latitude from Polaris

When you find latitude by Polaris what you see is what you get: your observed altitude is your latitude. Imagine you are walking from the North Pole to the Equator. At the North Pole, Polaris will be on your zenith and have an altitude of 90°. As you travel southwards it will sink one degree lower in the sky for every degree of latitude you journey south (see Figure 16.1). When you finally reach the equator, Polaris will have an altitude of zero.

Corrections for Polaris

Right now Polaris has a declination of about 89°12′. This means that it circles the true pole at a radius of 48 nautical miles. As it is so far away this circle is invisible to the naked eye but it does mean that if you measure the altitude of Polaris and take it as your latitude, you could be almost one degree out.

To find your true latitude by Polaris you must know where Polaris is on its daily circle. This is its hour angle and if you have no tables it can be found from the star clock.

A line joining the trailing stars in Cassiopeia and the Plough passes through Polaris and the true pole. Polaris is on the Cassiopeia side of the Pole. The easy corrections are:

1. If the line is at right angles to the horizon with Cassiopeia on top then the correction is −48′.

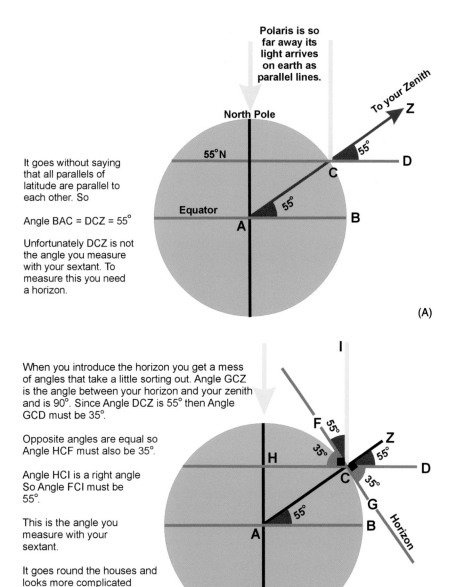

Polaris is so far away its light arrives on earth as parallel lines.

North Pole

55°N

It goes without saying that all parallels of latitude are parallel to each other. So

Angle BAC = DCZ = 55°

Unfortunately DCZ is not the angle you measure with your sextant. To measure this you need a horizon.

Equator

To your Zenith

(A)

When you introduce the horizon you get a mess of angles that take a little sorting out. Angle GCZ is the angle between your horizon and your zenith and is 90°. Since Angle DCZ is 55° then Angle GCD must be 35°.

Opposite angles are equal so Angle HCF must also be 35°.

Angle HCI is a right angle So Angle FCI must be 55°.

This is the angle you measure with your sextant.

It goes round the houses and looks more complicated than it is but now you know.

Horizon

(B)

16.1 Sextant Angles

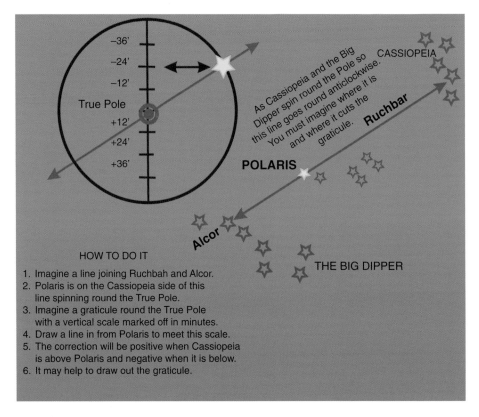

Inside the figure:

-36'
-24'
-12'
True Pole
+12'
+24'
+36'

As Cassiopeia and the Big Dipper spin round the Pole so this line goes round anticlockwise. You must imagine where it is and where it cuts the graticule.

CASSIOPEIA

Ruchbar

POLARIS

Alcor

THE BIG DIPPER

HOW TO DO IT

1. Imagine a line joining Ruchbah and Alcor.
2. Polaris is on the Cassiopeia side of this line spinning round the True Pole.
3. Imagine a graticule round the True Pole with a vertical scale marked off in minutes.
4. Draw a line in from Polaris to meet this scale.
5. The correction will be positive when Cassiopeia is above Polaris and negative when it is below.
6. It may help to draw out the graticule.

16.2 Polaris Correction

2. If the line is at right angles to the horizon with the Plough on top and Cassiopeia on the bottom, the correction is +48'.

It is more complicated when the line is at an angle to the horizon. Now you have to imagine where Polaris is on its journey round the Pole (see Figure 16.2). Once that is decided you have to add or subtract to find your true altitude.

Latitude from Circumpolar Stars

Circumpolar stars are stars that stay above your horizon and they can be used to find your latitude (shown in Figure 16.3).

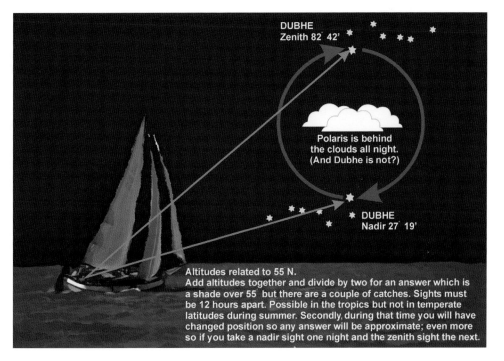

DUBHE
Zenith 82° 42'

Polaris is behind
the clouds all night.
(And Dubhe is not?)

DUBHE
Nadir 27° 19'

Altitudes related to 55 N.
Add altitudes together and divide by two for an answer which is
a shade over 55 but there are a couple of catches. Sights must
be 12 hours apart. Possible in the tropics but not in temperate
latitudes during summer. Secondly, during that time you will have
changed position so any answer will be approximate; even more
so if you take a nadir sight one night and the zenith sight the next.

16.3 Latitude by Circumpolar Stars

1. First identify your circumpolar star.

2. Measure its altitude when it is at its nadir. This is its lowest point in the sky
   and it is directly below the Pole.

3. Wait until it is at its zenith when it is directly above the Pole and measure its
   altitude again.

The average of your two readings, duly corrected, is the altitude of the Pole and
so your latitude. It does not matter if you do not know which star(s) you are using or
even their declination. The drawback is that the sights are 12 hours apart so you are
confined to circumpolar stars that are on the zenith (or nadir) at dusk and then at the
nadir (or zenith) around dawn.

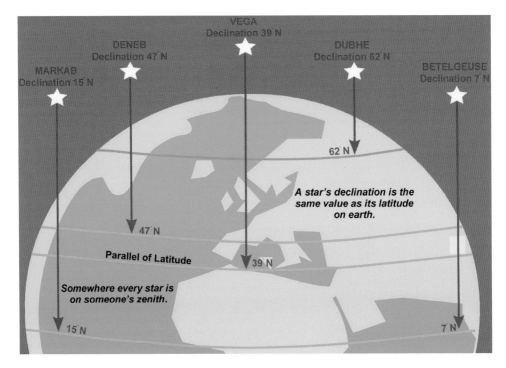

16.4 Zenith Stars

Zenith Stars

Since a star is at its zenith somewhere over the earth all day, every day this means that all stars circle the earth at their zenith (Figure 16.4). The angle that a star makes with the centre of the earth and the equator is called its declination. In earthly terms there is no difference between a star's declination and latitude. So when a star of a known declination is directly overhead then you know your latitude.

Imagine that you are sailing down your latitude to your chosen destination. In the northern hemisphere Polaris provides an easy latitude check but what if it is obscured, or if you are in the southern hemisphere?

Once you are on the latitude of your destination become familiar with stars passing through your zenith. It is not necessary to know them by name, only that they

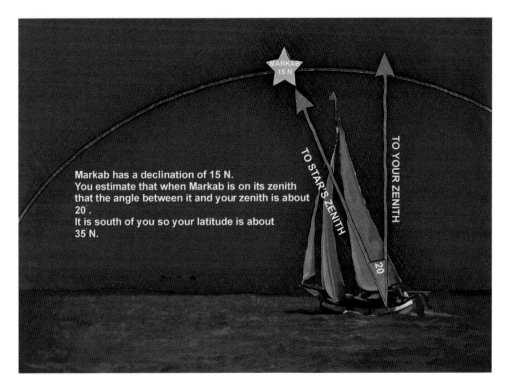

Markab has a declination of 15 N.
You estimate that when Markab is on its zenith
that the angle between it and your zenith is about
20 .
It is south of you so your latitude is about
35 N.

16.5 Latitude by ex-Meridian Stars

are your zenith stars and they confirm you are on course even if you do not know
their declination.

If a star whose declination you know is almost, but not exactly, on your zenith,
then you can try estimating the angle between it and your zenith (Figure 16.5). This will
not be easy and any answer is bound to be rough and ready but it may help to confirm
your latitude. If you reckon the star is 10° north of you then your latitude is 10° south of
its declination.

Longitude

Lunar Eclipses

Lunar Distances

Longitude by Time

Centuries ago it was realised that knowing your longitude at sea was a pearl beyond price and that the choice was between designing and building an accurate clock which would work afloat, or looking to the heavens to find the time.

People searched long and hard for other solutions. Henry Bond, in the 17th century, reckoned magnetic dip was the answer and said so in his book *Longitude Found*. Others suggested lines of anchored ships across the oceans, flashing lights onto clouds, measuring the height of tides, or inducing dogs to bark.

Lunar Eclipses

As far back as 160 BCE, the Greek astronomer Hipparchus had the idea of determining east/west positions by using lunar eclipses. This works but unfortunately there are only three or four lunar eclipses a year – not a lot of use when you want a daily fix.

Lunar Distances

Crafty navigators in the 15th and 16th centuries noted that as the moon circles the earth it changes its position at a constant rate relative to the sun and the stars. If the angle between the centre of the moon and a star or the centre of the sun could be measured, they reckoned they could calculate the time of the observation and then work out their longitude. They were right, but could not measure the angles involved accurately, and if they had been able to do so, they still lacked the data to do their sums.

Gathering this information was hard work. From 1689 to 1704 John Flamsteed, Britain's first Astronomer Royal, compiled tables for lunar distances. In 1756, Tobias

Mayer, keen to claim the British government's prize for finding longitude, sent his tables to the Board of Longitude. These were tested in 1761 on a voyage to St Helena. Longitude could always be found to within a degree but the report generously described the calculations for finding longitude by lunar distances as *laborious*.

There were a couple of problems preventing the adoption of lunar distances. Quadrants, the forerunners of today's sextants, only measure angles up to 90°. Lunar distances sometimes exceed this and in 1759 Captain John Campbell RN asked London instrument maker, John Bird, to make him a quadrant whose arc was one sixth of a circle (see Figure 17.1). So, the familiar sextant covering 120° of arc was born. Even so, the method did not gain popularity until the Nautical Almanac came out in 1767.

On his first Pacific voyage, James Cook sailed with a nautical almanac containing lunar distances. In his hands the results gave errors between 25–40'. This was as good as it got and Cook must have been delighted when Harrison finally produced his chronometer.

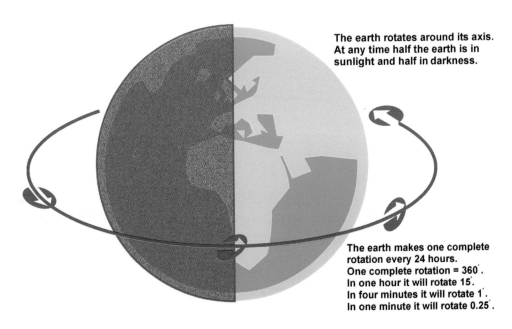

The earth rotates around its axis. At any time half the earth is in sunlight and half in darkness.

The earth makes one complete rotation every 24 hours.
One complete rotation = 360˚.
In one hour it will rotate 15˚.
In four minutes it will rotate 1˚.
In one minute it will rotate 0.25˚.

17.1 Time and Arc

Longitude by Time

The kindest way of describing finding longitude using the difference between local and Greenwich is 'approximate'. Small errors in time can produce surprisingly large errors in longitude. Still, it may be better than no longitude at all.

In 24 hours the earth turns through 360°. This means that in every hour it turns through 15° or that a difference of one degree of longitude equals four minutes of time (see Figure 17.2). Before leaving port, a ship's chronometer would have been set to GMT. Each day the time difference shown on the carefully cosseted chronometer, between GMT and local noon as noted from the sun, was calculated and turned into longitude east or west of Greenwich. Together with a noon latitude this would provide a noon fix.

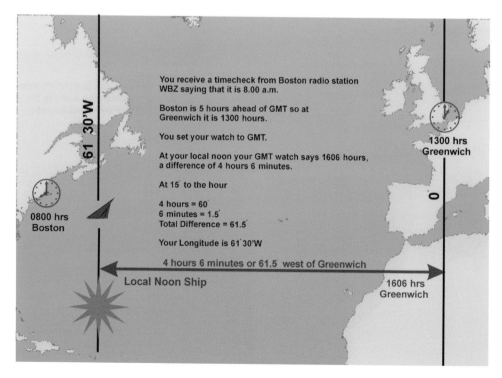

You receive a timecheck from Boston radio station WBZ saying that it is 8.00 a.m.

Boston is 5 hours ahead of GMT so at Greenwich it is 1300 hours.

You set your watch to GMT.

At your local noon your GMT watch says 1606 hours, a difference of 4 hours 6 minutes.

At 15' to the hour

4 hours = 60'
6 minutes = 1.5'
Total Difference = 61.5'

Your Longitude is 61 30'W

4 hours 6 minutes or 61.5 west of Greenwich

Local Noon Ship

1300 hrs Greenwich

1606 hrs Greenwich

0800 hrs Boston

61 30'W

17.2 Longitude by Time

If you have a watch set to Greenwich time and know its error, then use this method to produce a longitude, but treat its answers with healthy scepticism.

Radio Times

If you do not know GMT time then a suitable shortwave receiver allows you to pick up time signals and set a watch to GMT, but also commercial broadcasters on Am and Fm bands give time checks during the day and most give one at their noon. If they are using times other than GMT their times will have to be corrected to GMT, including allowances for summer times (see the example in Figure 17.2).

Plane sailing

Plane Sailing and Passage Planning

Traverse Tables Courses

For centuries, navigators thumbed through traverse tables using their course and distance sailed to find their latitude and longitude. They called this their 'daily work' (see Figure 18.1). This is 'plane' or 'raverse' sailing, and is based on the angles of a plane, right-angled triangle.

Back in the 14th century someone, knowing that trigonometry is not a seaman's strongest suit, worked out all the possible answers to all possible courses and distances and then published the answers as the world's first traverse tables. Nowadays you may find a copy in a forgotten corner of a nautical bookshop, but a cheap scientific calculator with trig functions lets you find the answers for yourself. It looks daunting when laid out on paper complete with explanations, but it is easier than jumping between columns in a book of traverse tables.

Plane Sailing and Passage Planning

Course to Steer

Without a course to steer all your effort in working out direction from the stars, sun and moon, and how to steer by the seat of your pants, is wasted. You need to know what direction to aim the bows rather than pointing towards the horizon and declaring, 'Thataway'!

If you know the latitude and longitude of both your start point and your destination then working out the course to steer is easy (see Figure 18.2).

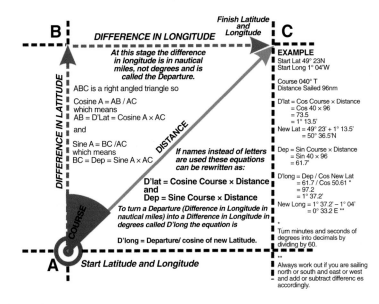

B
DIFFERENCE IN LONGITUDE

Finish Latitude and Longitude

C

At this stage the difference in longitude is in nautical miles, not degrees and is called the Departure.

ABC is a right angled triangle so

Cosine A = AB / AC
which means
AB = D'Lat = Cosine A × AC

and

Sine A = BC /AC
which means
BC = Dep = Sine A × AC

DISTANCE

COURSE

If names instead of letters are used these equations can be rewritten as:

D'lat = Cosine Course × Distance
and
Dep = Sine Course × Distance

To turn a Departure (Difference in Longitude in nautical miles) into a Difference in Longitude in degrees called D'long the equation is

D'long = Departure/ cosine of new Latitude.

DIFFERENCE IN LATITUDE

A **Start Latitude and Longitude**

EXAMPLE
Start Lat 49° 23N
Start Long 1° 04'W

Course 040° T
Distance Sailed 96nm

D'lat = Cos Course × Distance
= Cos 40 × 96
= 73.5
= 1° 13.5'
New Lat = 49° 23' + 1° 13.5'
= 50° 36.5'N

Dep = Sin Course × Distance
= Sin 40 × 96
= 61.7'

D'long = Dep / Cos New Lat
= 61.7 / Cos 50.61 *
= 97.2
= 1° 37.2'
New Long = 1° 37.2' – 1° 04'
= 0° 33.2 E **

*
Turn minutes and seconds of degrees into decimals by dividing by 60.

**
Always work out if you are sailing north or south and east or west and add or subtract differences accordingly.

18.1 Daily Work

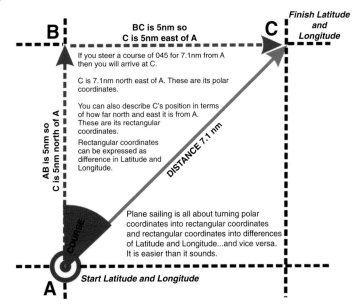

B

BC is 5nm so
C is 5nm east of A

Finish Latitude and Longitude

C

If you steer a course of 045 for 7.1nm from A then you will arrive at C.

C is 7.1nm north east of A. These are its polar coordinates.

You can also describe C's position in terms of how far north and east it is from A. These are its rectangular coordinates.

Rectangular coordinates can be expressed as difference in Latitude and Longitude.

AB is 5nm so
C is 5nm north of A

DISTANCE 7.1 nm

COURSE

Plane sailing is all about turning polar coordinates into rectangular coordinates and rectangular coordinates into differences of Latitude and Longitude...and vice versa. It is easier than it sounds.

A **Start Latitude and Longitude**

18.1a Plane Sailing

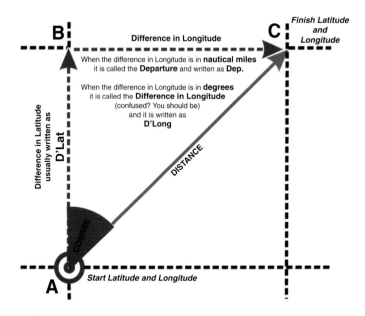

B ┆ **C** ┆ *Finish Latitude and Longitude*

Difference in Longitude

When the difference in Longitude is in **nautical miles** it is called the **Departure** and written as **Dep.**

When the difference in Longitude is in **degrees** it is called the **Difference in Longitude** (confused? You should be) and it is written as **D'Long**

Difference in Latitude usually written as **D'Lat**

DISTANCE

COURSE

A ┆ *Start Latitude and Longitude*

18.1b Plane Sailing

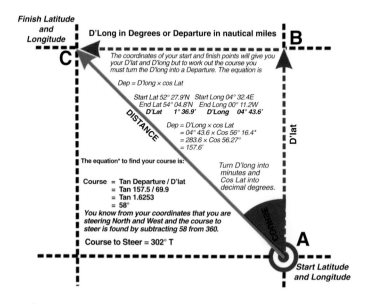

Finish Latitude and Longitude

D'Long in Degrees or Departure in nautical miles ┆ **B**

C

The coordinates of your start and finish points will give you your D'lat and D'long but to work out the course you must turn the D'long into a Departure. The equation is

$Dep = D'long \times cos \ Lat$

Start Lat 52° 27.9'N   Start Long 04° 32.4E
End Lat 54° 04.8'N   End Long 00° 11.2W
D'Lat   1° 36.9'   D'Long   04° 43.6'

$Dep = D'Long \times cos \ Lat$
$= 04° \ 43.6 \times Cos \ 56° \ 16.4"$
$= 283.6 \times Cos \ 56.27°$
$= 157.6'$

DISTANCE

D'lat

The equation* to find your course is:

Turn D'long into minutes and Cos Lat into decimal degrees.

Course = Tan Departure / D'lat
= Tan 157.5 / 69.9
= Tan 1.6253
= 58°

You know from your coordinates that you are steering North and West and the course to steer is found by subtracting 58 from 360.

Course to Steer = 302° T

COURSE

A

Start Latitude and Longitude

18.2 Course to Steer

154

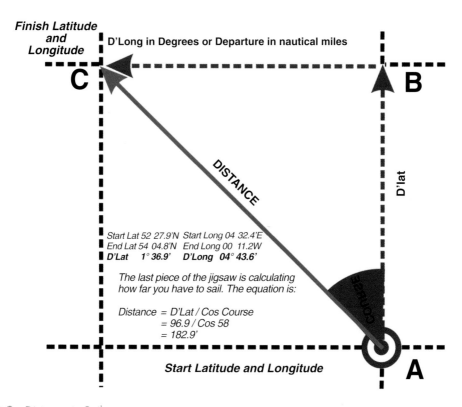

Finish Latitude and Longitude

D'Long in Degrees or Departure in nautical miles

C

B

DISTANCE

D'lat

Start Lat 52 27.9'N   Start Long 04 32.4'E
End Lat 54 04.8'N   End Long 00 11.2W
D'Lat   1° 36.9'   D'Long 04° 43.6'

The last piece of the jigsaw is calculating how far you have to sail. The equation is:

Distance = D'Lat / Cos Course
= 96.9 / Cos 58
= 182.9'

COURSE

Start Latitude and Longitude

A

18.3 Distance to Sail

Distance to Sail

The second question is, how far? Once again, traverse tables provide the answer (see Figure 18.3). Be careful, plane sailing is good up to about 400 nautical miles, beyond which the answers become increasingly doubtful.

Traverse Tables Courses

Although you can enter the courses in 360° notation into your calculator sometimes it will automatically acquire a minus sign. This is because the right-angled triangle you are solving could be in any one of the four quadrants making up a compass. The answer

QUADRANTAL NOTATION	DEGREES	QUADRANTAL NOTATION	DEGREES
NORTH	360	NORTH	000
N 5° W	355	N 5° E	005
N 10° W	350	N 10° E	010
N 15° W	345	N 15° E	015
N 20° W	340	N 20° E	020
N 25° W	335	N 25° E	025
N 30° W	330	N 30° E	030
N 35° W	325	N 35° E	035
N 40° W	320	N 40° E	040
N 45° W	315	N 45° E	045
N 50° W	310	N 50° E	050
N 55° W	305	N 55° E	055
N 60° W	300	N 60° E	060
N 65° W	295	N 65° E	065
N 70° W	290	N 70° E	070
N 75° W	285	N 75° E	075
N 80° W	280	N 80° E	080
N 86° W	275	N 86° E	085
WEST	270	EAST	090
S 85° W	265	S 85° E	095
S 80° W	260	S 80° E	100
S 75° W	255	S 75° E	105
S 70° W	250	S 70° E	110

18.4 Quadrantal Notation (*continued overleaf*)

QUADRANTAL	DEGREES	QUADRANTAL	DEGREES
S 65° W	245	S 65° E	115
S 60° W	240	S 60° E	120
S 55° W	235	S 55° E	125
S 50° W	230	S 50° E	130
S 45° W	225	S 45° E	135
S 40° W	220	S 40° E	140
S 35° W	215	S 35° E	145
S 30° W	210	S 30° E	150
S 25° W	205	S 25° E	155
S 20° W	200	S 20° E	160
S 15° W	195	S 15° E	165
S 10° W	190	S 10° E	170
S 5° W	185	S 5° E	175
SOUTH	180	SOUTH	180

A course of 030° could be

$$N\ 30°E = 30° \text{ east from north} = 000 + 30 = 030°$$
$$S\ 30°E = 30° \text{ east from south} = 180 - 30 = 150°$$
$$N30°W = 30° \text{ west from north} = 360 - 30 = 330°$$
$$S\ 30°W = 30° \text{ west from south} = 180 + 30 = 210°$$

18.4 *(Continued)*

is the same for each quadrant. Traditionally, courses used to solve the traverse are described as between 0–90° east or west from north or south. You must work out which quadrant your answer is in and turn it into 360° notation. There is no snappy formula to provide the answer. You must work it out (see the tables in Figure 18.4).

Chartmaking

Home-Made Charts

Charts for Coastal Passages

Representing our three-dimensional world on two-dimensional paper warps reality. The distortion used on a particular map is called its projection. In 1569 Gerard Kramer, known professionally as Gerardus Mercator, invented the projection that bears his name.

Mercator's projection was an instant hit with navigators because it allowed them to draw their courses as straight lines. The secret behind this is that a Mercator chart thinks the world is a cylinder, and lines of longitude, instead of meeting at the poles, are parallel to each other. They do this by growing further and further apart as you travel north or south from the equator (see Mercator charts in Figure 19.1). This is only possible because the latitude scale varies while the longitude scale is constant. Every single second of latitude is slightly larger than its predecessor, whereas in real life, or on a globe, they are equal. Mercator never explained how he drew his charts. It was 30 years after his first chart that an Oxford don called Edward Wright worked out the maths behind the Mercator projection.

Home-made Charts

If you do not have paper charts on board then you will need to draw one. This is a very old skill. In the days when there was terra incognita, explorers drew their charts as they sailed. You can do the same.

First decide on the scale. The longitude scale is constant and the ratio of longitude to latitude is 1: secant of your latitude. A secant is the inverse of a cosine, or one divided by the cosine of your latitude. If you are in latitude 50° north or south then you need the secant of 50° or 1 / Cos 50°. The answer is 1.5557. In other words the ratio

If you were drawing a Mercator chart of the world where 1′ Longitude equals 1cm then at the Equator 1′ Latitude equals 1cm but as you move north or south the latitude scale grows exponentially.

At 0° N/S	1′ Longitude equals 1cm	1′ Latitude equals 1cm
At 10°N/S	1′ Longitude equals 1cm	1′ Latitude equals 1.015 cm
At 20° N/S	1′ Longitude equals 1cm	1′ Latitude equals 1.064 cm
At 30° N/S	1′ Longitude equals 1cm	1′ Latitude equals 1.154 cm
At 50° N/S	1′ Longitude equals 1cm	1′Latitude equals 1.556 cm
At 80° N/S	1′ Longitude equals 1cm	1′ Latitude equals 5.759 cm
At 89° N/S	1′ Longitude equals 1cm	1′ Latitude equals 57.299 cm
At 89.90°N/S	1′ Longitude equals 1cm	1′ Latitude equals 572.958 cm
At 90° N/S	1′ Longitude equals 1cm	1′ Latitude equals Infinity

19.1   Mercator Charts Latitude Versus Longitude

between longitude and latitude is 1:1.5557 and on your hand-drawn chart it means:

1′ of longitude = 1mm, cm or whatever unit you chose.

And:

1′ of latitude = 1.5557 mm, cm or whatever unit you chose. You must use the same units for both latitude and longitude.

If you are unable to work out the secant of your latitude then decide upon a suitable longitude scale and find the latitude scale graphically (Figures 19.2 to 19.5 show you how).

It is best to keep home-made charts to one degree of latitude, especially if you are sailing in high latitudes where small changes in latitude can have a disproportionate effect on scale. In the real world Australia is far larger than Greenland, but not on a Mercator map.

Charts for Coastal Passages

Blank charts are fine in the middle of nowhere but when you are approaching the coast, some detail ashore will show you how close your plot puts you to land and whether or not the course you have chosen will bring you to harbour.

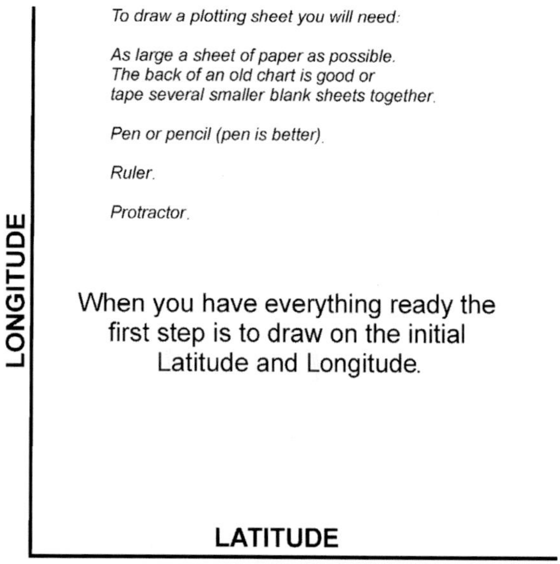

To draw a plotting sheet you will need:

As large a sheet of paper as possible.
The back of an old chart is good or
tape several smaller blank sheets together.

Pen or pencil (pen is better).

Ruler.

Protractor.

**When you have everything ready the
first step is to draw on the initial
Latitude and Longitude.**

LONGITUDE

LATITUDE

19.2 Drawing a Plotting Sheet
Step 1

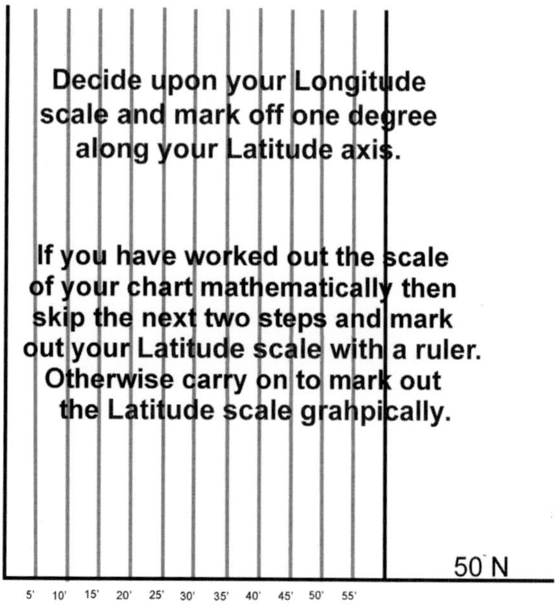

**Decide upon your Longitude
scale and mark off one degree
along your Latitude axis.**

**If you have worked out the scale
of your chart mathematically then
skip the next two steps and mark
out your Latitude scale with a ruler.
Otherwise carry on to mark out
the Latitude scale grahpically.**

50 N

5'   10'   15'   20'   25'   30'   35'   40'   45'   50'   55'

19.3 Drawing a Plotting Sheet
Step 2

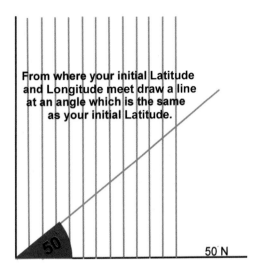

19.4 Drawing a Plotting Sheet Step 3

From where your initial Latitude and Longitude meet draw a line at an angle which is the same as your initial Latitude.

50°

50 N

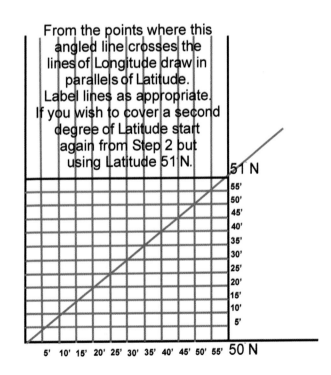

19.5 Drawing a Plotting Sheet Step 4

From the points where this angled line crosses the lines of Longitude draw in parallels of Latitude. Label lines as appropriate. If you wish to cover a second degree of Latitude start again from Step 2 but using Latitude 51 N.

51 N
55'
50'
45'
40'
35'
30'
25'
20'
15'
10'
5'

5' 10' 15' 20' 25' 30' 35' 40' 45' 50' 55' 50 N

There is a lot of information you can add to your chart. You can begin by inserting your waypoints. Next, you can try sketching in the coast as you remember it. If you have a pilot or Almanac on board you will have a treasure trove of information including the coordinates of ports, lights, buoys, and hazards, which you can plot on your chart.

Signs of landfall

Waves

   Birds

   Clouds

   Aircraft

   Commercial Radio Stations

   Shore Lights

   Shipping

Before land is seen there will be signs that it is close. Not all will come into view at the same time but their appearance, more or less on schedule, confirms your plan is coming together.

Waves

The stronger the wind, the longer it blows from the same direction, and the greater its fetch, the higher the waves (see table in Figure 20.1). Add swell from other winds, currents, depth of water, rain (heavy rain can flatten waves) and, should you be that far north or south, the chance of ice, and what should be a simple relationship between wind and wave becomes very complicated.

Wave Height

The significant wave height is the average of the highest one third of waves. Note the height of 150 waves, take the heights of the highest 50 and find their average. Judging the height of waves from a small boat at sea is extremely difficult (see Figure 20.2) and for the yachtsman, calculating the significant wave height can be a fruitless exercise.

Wavelength and Speed

The speed at which a wave travels depends on whether it is in deep or shallow water. Deep water is water deeper than half the wavelength.

Bft wind force	Maximum wave height with unlimited duration and fetch	Duration of wind to produce 50% of maximum wave height	Duration of wind to produce 75% of maximum wave height	Duration of wind to produce 90% of maximum wave height	Fetch with unlimited duration of wind to produce 50% of max wave height	Fetch with unlimited duration of wind to produce 75% of max wave height	Fetch with unlimited duration of wind to produce 90% of max wave height
3	2 ft	1.5 hrs	5 hrs	8 hrs	3 nm	13 nm	25 nm
5	8 ft	3.5 hrs	8 hrs	12 hrs	10 nm	30 nm	60 nm
7	20 ft	5.5 hrs	11 hrs	21 hrs	22 nm	75 nm	150 nm
9	40 ft	7 hrs	16 hrs	25 hrs	55 nm	150 nm	280 nm
11	70 ft	9 hrs	19 hrs	32 hrs	85 nm	200 nm	450 nm

20.1 Wave Height and Wind Force, Duration and Fetch

For deep-water waves the equation is:

$$WAVELENGTH = 1.56 \times wave\ period\ squared.$$

The speed of a wave is found by:

$$WAVE\ SPEED = 1.25 \times square\ root\ of\ wavelength\ in\ metres.$$

Shallow Water

In shallow water, both wavelength and speed decrease, and height and steepness (wavelength divided by height) increase. Shallow water waves are affected by:

- **Reflection:** When waves bounce off an obstacle like a rock or a reef back into the oncoming wave front.

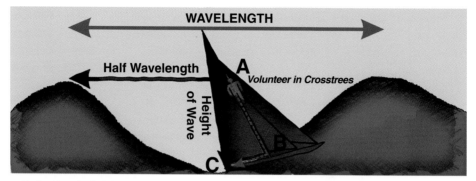

WAVELENGTH

Half Wavelength

A *Volunteer in Crosstrees*

Height of Wave

B

C

Estimating the height of waves is very difficult. A reliable method is to have a volunteer in the crosstrees. When he is level with the crest of a wave you can calculate its height using Pythagorus' theorem. In calmer weather the volunteer can be closer to the deck.

The most important parameters in describing a wave are its Period (P), Speed (S) and Length (L). If you know two of these you can find the third. The basic equation is:

Wave Length = Speed × Period.

Deep water is water over half a wave length deep. Shallow water is under half a wavelength. In shallow water everything except the period changes. Wave Length and Speed decrease and Height increases.

In oceans, waves break when the height to wavelength ratio is about 1:7. In shallow water it is between 1:1.5 to 1:1.25.

20.2

- **Diffraction:** When waves squeeze together as they pass through the entrance to a bay or a harbour, then spread out again.

- **Refraction:** Where part of the wave is in shallow water and the rest is in deep water. The part in shallow water slows down but the remainder keeps going with the result that the wave pivots round the portion in shallow water.

Reflection, diffraction and refraction can happen all at once and the result, even on a calm day, can be a very unfriendly sea.

Breaking Waves

In deep water waves begin to break when the ratio of wave height to wavelength is about 1:7. In shallow water it is usual to assume that they begin breaking when the depth of water is about 1.25 times the wave height.

Swell

Swells are waves created by winds outside your sea area. They are travelling through and have nothing to do with the winds that you are experiencing or the waves those winds create. Unless they hit an obstacle, swells maintain their direction, and in theory, if the helmsman keeps them at a constant angle to the boat, they are a simple aid to maintaining course.

Sadly, in practice this is not the case. Swells often come from more than one direction at the same time and then you have to identify waves generated by local winds. Unless there is one dominant, very obvious wave train, using swells for direction for any length of time is extremely difficult.

Waves in Soundings

On a continental shelf wavelength shortens and the waves steepen. Closer to land the colour of the sea may change and rubbish may appear in the water.

If you are approaching a steep-to coast with no beach to absorb the energy of breaking waves, then when a swell hits the coast it is reflected back out to sea (see Figure 20.3 and Figure 20.4). This creates a cross swell which may be detectable some distance offshore. Before acting on this you must be sure that there is no other possible source for the cross swell and answer the question why, if you are within a handful of miles of a cliffy coast, you have not seen land.

On sand and shingle beaches waves hit the beach at an angle but their backwash runs straight down the beach taking the beach material with it. These beaches absorb the force of breaking seas and there is less chance of detecting reflected waves out at sea.

When swells approach an isolated obstruction such as an island, they try to wrap themselves around it (Figure 20.5). The first sign is the reflected swell from the up-swell

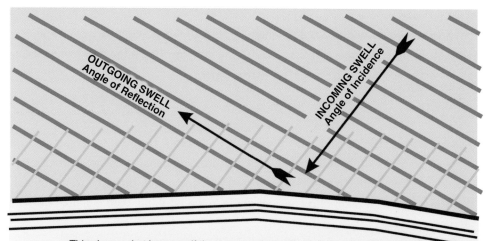

This shows what happens if there are vertical cliffs plunging into deep water.
If there is a shelving beach the incoming swell curves round trying to hit the shore
at right angles. The further offshore the shelving extends the more the incoming
swell swings round.
A beach absorbs the energy of the incoming swell. The gentler the slope of the beach and the
further offshore it extends the more energy it absorbs. When this happens there is often a line of
offshore breakers and the reflected swell will peter out close inshore.
The depth of water will affect how far the reflected swell goes offshore. It will go further
at high tide than low especially if there is a wave cut shelf. (Figure 20.4)

20.3 Relected Waves

Diagrams always show refracting waves swinging round like guardsmen on parade. In the real world
refraction is largely controlled by the shape and composition of the bottom and waves can wander about
like drunks after the bar has closed. This may not be apparent from seawards. There will little or no
reflection from this type of beach and in thick weather the first sign of approaching land may be the
sudden appearance of swell in an otherwise calm sea or an abrupt shortening of wavelength and
increase in wave height if there is a sea running. You may be very close to land when this happens
and safety lies in heading back out to sea immediately.

SWELL LINE STARTS ABOUT HERE

SHINGLE BEACH ABSORBS
WAVE ENERGY

REFRACTING WAVEFRONT

20.3b Wave Refraction

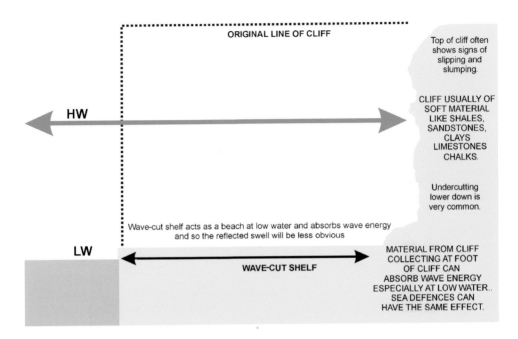

20.4 Wave Cut Shelf

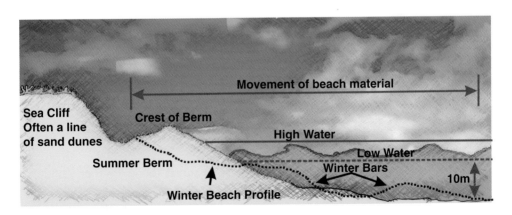

20.4b A Sand and Shingle Beach

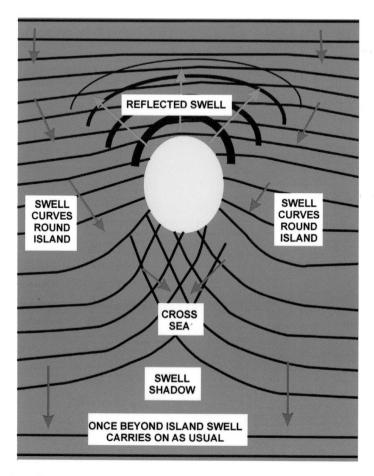

20.5 Island Swell

side of the island creating a cross sea. Then the swell curves round the island and meets itself to create another cross sea just beyond the lee of the island. The range at which these often subtle signs can be picked up varies with the swell and the size of the island. A large island will have a greater effect than a small island. The original swell may be confused by cross swells from other sources. You could be looking at a babel of waves that make no sense at all.

Birds

Very few seabirds live at sea. Most nest on land and fly out in the morning to their fishing grounds and fly home at the end of the working day. Their flight paths are a good indication of where land lies. Flocks of birds feeding at sea are probably a sign that land is within a maximum of 50 nautical miles or a fishing boat within 50 metres.

Clouds

During the day, land heats up faster than sea. The warm air over the land rises and is replaced by moist air drawn in from the sea, which in turn is warmed by the land and rises. The rising air cools and the moisture it picked up over the sea chills out as a cloud.

If there is no wind then this cloud sits over the land. On windless days the warm air will continue to rise after it has lost its moisture. This can split the cloud into two and then it sits, like bushy eyebrows, either side of the island.

If a wind is blowing, the top of the cloud may stream downwind. Sometimes the entire cloud may be blown downwind, only to be replaced by a new cloud forming over the island.

Sometimes the base of the cloud reflects the colour of the land below, taking on a greenish tinge if the land is wooded, or a light bluish-green tinge if there is a lagoon.

Clouds are visible at great distances. Divide them into High Clouds, Middle Clouds and Low Clouds (Figure 20.6) and look for:

- Stationary clouds. Many books have pictures showing a single cloud sitting over a solitary island. Real life is complicated by the presence of other, very similar looking clouds that have nothing to do with the island. These move with the wind. The island cloud is the one standing still.

- 'Eyebrows' either side of an out-of-sight island.

- Clouds with their tops streaming downwind when every other cloud moves downwind in its entirety. This is caused by the stationary cloud continuously reforming above the island as its top blows away.

Cloud Level	Height	Compostion	Cloud Type
High Clouds	Above 20,000 ft (6100 m)	Mainly ice crystals	Cirrus, Cirrocumulus, Cirrostratus
Middle Clouds	6500–20000 ft (2000–6100 m)	Mostly water droplets although higher regions may contain ice particles	Altocumulus, Altostratus,
Low Clouds	Up to 6500 ft (2000 m)	Entirely water droplets.	Stratocumulus, Nimbostratus,Cumulus, Cumulosnimbus

20.6

- Clouds always forming in the same place. The wind may be strong enough to blow the island cloud away entirely but another forms in its place. It should be obvious but if there are other clouds around it is only noticeable if you watch the clouds carefully.

- Clouds whose base is a different colour to other clouds. While this is a good indication of land it is really just a sign that something other than deep water is reflecting light into the cloud base. This 'something else' could be a reef.

Aircraft

Contrails high in the sky can be a useful guide to direction. Trans-oceanic aircraft tend to follow great circle routes and their final destination may not be in exactly the direction they are pointing, but they do fly between landmasses.

If you are making an island landfall then aircraft landing on the island can point the way, especially at night when their lights are visible from 30 or more miles away as they circle the sky like stars gone walkabout.

Commercial Radio Stations

A simple transistor radio can not only warn of approaching land, it tells you where it is. When you begin receiving programmes, rotate the set horizontally so that even with the

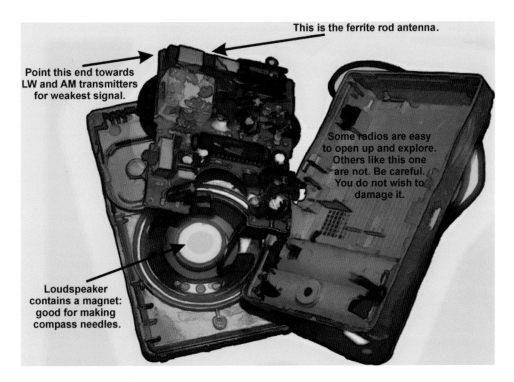

This is the ferrite rod antenna.

Point this end towards
LW and AM transmitters
for weakest signal.

Some radios are easy
to open up and explore.
Others like this one
are not. Be careful.
You do not wish to
damage it.

Loudspeaker
contains a magnet:
good for making
compass needles.

20.7 A Transistor Radio

volume at full almost nothing is heard. The ferrite rod antenna in the set is now pointing at the transmitter, which is almost certainly on land (see Figure 20.7).

Long wave signals can be picked up at about 400 nautical miles, medium wave at about 100 nautical miles and VHF (Fm) signals around 30 nautical miles. Signal strength should increase as you approach land. The easiest way to determine this is to keep the volume setting constant and listen for the sound growing louder. If the signal strength decreases then either the batteries are flat or you are sailing in the wrong direction. This works. Japanese pilots tuned into Radio Honolulu to find Pearl Harbor.

Shore Lights

Like the cloud base reflecting the colour of the land underneath, shore lights also light up the cloud base and are visible from many miles offshore. The bigger the settlement the bigger the area of cloud lit up. If there are no clouds the loom of shore lights can be seen from miles offshore. Be careful. Shore lights may be some distance inland. Do not approach too closely until you are sure where the sea stops and the land begins.

Shipping

As you near land there is a better-than-even chance that you will cross one or more shipping lanes. As their position is known, this can confirm your DR. Offshore from most major harbours, particularly if they are upriver, there are large-ship anchorages, which provide another excellent position check. In some areas such as the North Sea you will find oil or gas platforms. These carry numbers and their position appears in pilots and almanacs.

Accuracy

Course Errors

Plotting Positions

There is no answer to the question, *What degree of accuracy can I expect?* You always work with approximations. Figures should be rounded to one decimal place, or even the nearest whole number. Anything else creates a false impression of precision.

Course Errors

Steering within 10° either side of your course is good, but after 60 miles you could be 10 miles off course and after 1200 miles you could be 200 miles off course. In the real world tides turn, winds shift and helmsmen wake up. Errors balance out and the course you finally make good is usually pretty near the course you wanted.

Be aware that when tacking, you are zigzagging across your mean line of advance and errors made on one tack are cancelled by those on the next tack, but on a run you hold the same course for long periods and errors can accumulate.

Plotting Positions

Although you may not know your exact course and speed you have a good idea of their range. You have been sailing due east and know you have made four to five knots and steered between 085° and 095°. There is a choice how you plot this information on a chart. The simplest is take the mean of course and speed, draw a course of 090° for 4.5 nautical miles and put a circle of error around your DR position. Its diameter reflects your confidence. If you are 90% confident it would be a small circle, say half a mile across; at 80% it would be a mile (see Figure 21.1).

Circle of Error
Your actual position
is somewhere inside
this circle. Unless
there is a hazard nearby
accept your DR plot.

090˚ for 4.5nm

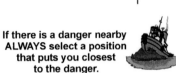

If there is a danger nearby
ALWAYS select a position
that puts you closest
to the danger.

21.1 Circles of Error

You could make two plots. One uses the minimum values of course, speed, tide, current and leeway; the other the maximum values. Each plot has its own circle of error. Hopefully they will overlap. If there is no nearby hazard, your assumed position will be in the middle of the overlap and can be plotted by taking the mean of your values (see Figure 21.2).

Finally, you can reject the circle of error in favour of the Quad of Uncertainty. This accepts that you stay within the maximum and minimum of the estimated courses steered and the distances sailed, and the result places you inside a box (see Figure 21.3).

On average
Whenever possible, take the average of several measurements. If one measurement is wildly different from the others then it is probably wrong, and should be discarded.

One Step at a Time
It helps to break a passage into as many legs as possible, the more the better. If possible each leg should end at a position that gives you a fix. This way you do not make one long voyage but a series of shorter passages, each starting from a known position.

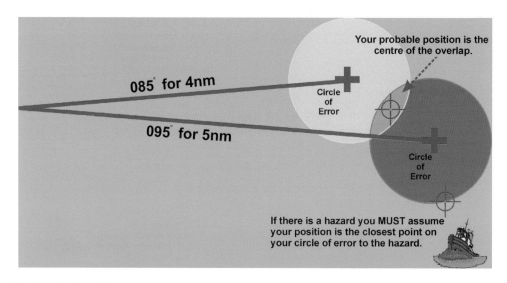

21.2 Circles of Error

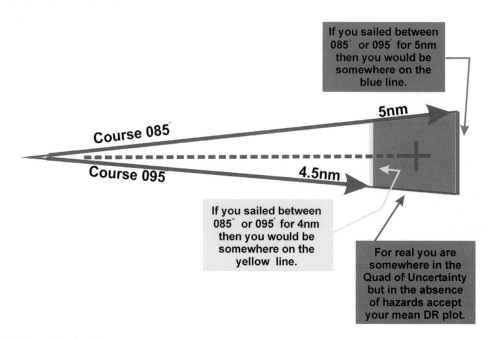

21.3 Quad of Uncertainty

Cross Checking

When crossing the North Sea or sailing back to England from northern France there may seem to be no place for celestial navigation. Wrong. A latitude from the noon sun or Polaris should pass through your DR position (Figure 21.4). If it does not, then it is back to the drawing board.

Checking It Out

With GPS we happily rely on a single source of information. Without GPS, the rule is that a solitary source will not provide a trustworthy answer. Different sources should tell the same story even if they tell it at different times and in their own way. The first sign of

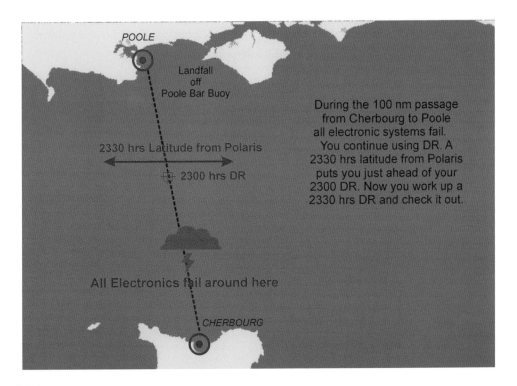

POOLE

Landfall
off
Poole Bar Buoy

2330 hrs Latitude from Polaris

2300 hrs DR

During the 100 nm passage from Cherbourg to Poole all electronic systems fail. You continue using DR. A 2330 hrs latitude from Polaris puts you just ahead of your 2300 DR. Now you work up a 2330 hrs DR and check it out.

All Electronics fail around here

CHERBOURG

21.4

approaching land could be when you pick up long wave radio programmes. Later when you start receiving Fm programmes you could begin looking for clouds building up over an island or along the coast. Soon you would expect to see seabirds, perhaps shipping lanes, aircraft losing height for landing, changes in the swell, flotsam both natural and man-made and finally the appearance of inshore traffic and local fishermen.

The Crash Bag Navigator snaps up every snippet of information and uses them as pieces of a jigsaw that shows the world around the boat, and its place in it. This is an ever-changing picture, modified whenever any new piece of information comes to hand. Keeping this plot up to date is a full-time job. The electronic navigator knows only what his screens tell him. His position is a dot or a series of figures on a screen. It is not something he knows or something that he has worked out and can prove. It is something he is told and must unquestioningly accept. Deprived of his solitary source of information an electronic navigator stops navigating. A Crash Bag Navigator who loses one source of information carries on. His supply of information has diminished, not dried up. He may be uncertain of his position but he is never lost.

Index

Lifeboats

' Flat calm or force 10. I always wear one.'

Whether they're training or out on a shout, RNLI crew members always wear lifejackets. It's a rule informed by years of experience. They know that, whatever the weather, the sea's extremely unpredictable – and can turn at a moment's notice. They see people caught out all the time. People who've risked, or even lost their lives as a result. The fact is, a lifejacket will buy you vital time in the water – and could even save your life. But only if you're wearing it.

For advice on choosing a lifejacket and how to wear it correctly, call us on 0800 328 0600 (UK) or 1800 789 589 (RoI) or visit our website rnli.org.uk/seasafety/lifejackets

Useless unless worn